```
792.0222 L541
Lemay, Anne,
    Dog days and winter ways
  : skits to promote reading
```

Dog Days & Winter Ways

Skits to Promote Reading All Year Long

By Anne Lemay

Alleyside Press

Fort Atkinson, Wisconsin

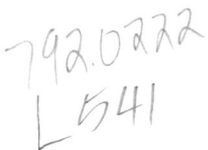

Published by Alleyside Press, an imprint of Highsmith Press

Highsmith Press
W5527 Highway 106
P.O. Box 800
Fort Atkinson, Wisconsin 53538-0800

© Anne Lemay, 1994

Cover by Frank Neu
Author's photo by CJ Barron-Douglas

All rights reserved. Printed in the United States of America
Except as permitted under the United States Copyright Act of 1976, no part of this publication may be reproduced or distributed in any form or by any means, or stored in a database or retrieval system, without the prior written permission of the publisher.

The paper used in this publication meets the minimum requirements of American National Standard for Information Science — Permanence of Paper for Printed Library Material. ANSI/NISO Z39.48-1992.

Library of Congress Cataloging in Publication

Lemay, Anne, 1953–

    Dog days & winter ways: skits to promote reading all year long / by Anne Lemay.

       p.   cm.

    ISBN 0-917846-40-0 (alk. paper) : $9.95

     1. Amateur plays--United States. 2. American drama. 3. Children--United States--Bokks and reading--Drama. 4. Advertising--United States--Libraries. I. Title. II. Dog days and winter ways.

PN6119.9.L46 1994

792'.0222--dc20   94-7904

                                       CIP

ISBN 0-917846-40-0

KENT FREE LIBRARY

Contents

Introduction *1*
1. Planning Your Production *3*
2. Rehearsals *7*
3. Acting: Quick Study for the Novice *13*
4. Writing Your Own Skits *19*
5. Reading Pleasures, Deep Sea Treasures *25*
6. Trouble With Magic *29*
7. Station W-Library *35*
8. Three Ring Reading *39*
   Appendix A: Contacting Performance Sites *45*
   Appendix B: Stage Areas *47*
   Appendix C: Glossary *49*

Introduction

"Hey, I saw you at school! You were the pirate!"

Actually, I was and still am a librarian in Children's Services at the local public library, a.k.a. "the rabbit," "the pirate," "the magician," "the clown," and a complete cast of other characters. The child who made this comment saw a skit I performed with another librarian in our local public school system to promote the library's summer reading club. We're glad we hear lots of comments like this one, and are pleased to know the children remember our message—as the comments continue through the summer and on into the following school year.

Why use a skit?

Many children today have little opportunity to experience "live theater," yet my colleagues and I have found it a very effective way to promote reading.

In a way, skits can be used as a type of "live commercial." The goal of the typical commercial is to sell something to the viewer, usually in an entertaining format. As a promotional tool, commercials have proven to be very effective. In the library, you can use it to promote something positive and educational.

Your goal in using this entertaining format may be to promote the summer reading club, any other reading program that needs a little public attention or even library's services in general. Ultimately, all of the characters in these skits end up in the library, which is exactly what you want the children to do, too. Feel free to edit, change, adapt, and revise to suit your own purpose and locale.

You may want to jump right into your favorite skit and start planning right now, however, if the idea of performing in front of real people is new to you, if you have cold feet just thinking about it, or even if you'd just like some suggestions of more ways to use the skits in your school or library, take a look at chapters 1–3. If a bit of the bard runs through your blood, take a look at chapter 4 for a glimpse at how I write the skits and for advice on how to do it yourself.

If, as Shakespeare said, all the world's a stage—take advantage of it! Happy reading, happy writing, happy acting—happy promoting.

1
Planning Your Production

Once you have chosen the theme for the library's reading club, you're ready to choose a skit, recruit actors, and set up a performance schedule.

Finding the right skit

Choosing a skit is easy if your theme fits one of the skits in this book, but a little creative thinking will help you adapt any one of these to your situation. It's obvious that the pirate skit might be adapted to any ocean, beach, or treasure theme, but if your theme is something like "Explore New Worlds With Reading," the same basic skit might be performed with two aliens instead of two pirates, or with two sailors travelling with Columbus or Henry Hudson. Two aliens might just as easily be radio broadcasters reporting on Earth's Olympics. What if two cave men were reporting on the Dinosaur Olympics? Not historically accurate, but certain to draw attention. A plug for library research can easily be worked into that one.

Casting

You've chosen the skit and adapted it to your circumstances, if necessary (See chapter 4 for suggestions to help you do that.). The next step is casting.

In many libraries there is only one children's librarian, so if you're doing one of the skits in this book, you'll need help. There may be a willing circulation assistant. The students would probably love to see the school principal hamming it up! You may be able to cooperate with a librarian from a nearby school or town and perform together in both places. You may choose to direct two students in the skit. Teachers perform in front of a class every day. A teacher in your building may be a fine fellow actor in a skit, with the experience and dash necessary to make the skit successful.

Assuming you have your choice of local actors, what should you be looking for in casting a skit?

Keeping the characters in mind, look for someone who has a high energy level and a voice that will carry. Previous stage experience is helpful, though not essential. Even professional actors get last-minute butterflies, so expect someone with less experience to have a certain amount of stage fright. Someone who has a vivid imagination and expresses himself or herself creatively might bring those qualities to the stage.

Another quality to look for is the ability to work well with others. Since the creativity of the theater is dependent on the joint efforts of those involved, a flexible attitude, the ability to take direction from another, and mutual respect for each other's efforts is important.

Students as actors: Holding auditions

If students are your choice as actors, you will still want a high energy level and voices that will carry, as well as finding actors with the ability to perform in front of a large group of people. It may be harder to find students with these qualities, though certainly not impossible. It is difficult to judge the abilities of students as actors ahead of time, since the best reader may not be the best at bringing a character to life on the stage, and even the "class cut-up," as bold as he or she is, may not be able to play any other role on stage.

It is a good idea to hold auditions for your student actors. This will give you a chance to test their abilities before committing yourself to casting the roles. Keep your characters in mind during the audition process, and if at all possible, cast the students according to their personalities (called "type casting" in the theater). For example, a bossy know-it-all type of person (like the character Lucy in the Peanuts comic strips will usually play a bossy know-it-all character very well, and a sweet, shy person will most likely do an excellent job as the "sweet young thing."

The purpose of auditions is to learn as much as possible about how well each potential actor is suited to a role, and how well each actor performs, takes direction, and expresses his or her imagination. Bear in mind that "Jane Smith" on the stage may not be the same "Jane Smith" you see in the classroom. Some people become terribly shy on stage, while others open up and become more expressive. Many are somewhere in between and need your help and direction to grow to their full potential.

Remember that the ability to read well doesn't necessarily mean that the student can act well. Sometimes what you see is all you'll ever get, which means that the skit may not grow to a performance level. Look at physical appearance and how the student moves. Can the student stand still, yet not look as stiff as a board? Does he or she move comfortably on the stage? Is this student's physical appearance well-suited to the character? Bear in mind that the unexpected can add to the humor, such as a "baby" being larger than its "mother." Listen to the student's voice. Is it a monotone? Does it sound artificial? Is the student reciting? When the actor speaks, the words should mean something. If the potential actor recites (or sounds artificial), these are warning flags, but again, acting ability can't be determined solely from reading skills.

Theatrical improvisation

The "Improvisation" is a game used in acting classes to help student actors loosen up, think quickly, and stay in character. Using an improvisation at auditions will let you determine how your actors relate to one another. You may work with the whole group or with two or three actors at a time.

If you are working with elementary school students, a folktale will easily lend itself to improvisation. For instance, to use the story of "Hansel and Gretel," put on some quiet music or an environmental tape of woodland sounds, and tell the group that they are walking in an enchanted forest. Encourage them to walk all around the space you are using, whether you are limited to a stage or have a whole room. Help them along with a description, such as, "You are all alone, and the dark trees tower over you, branches are reaching for you like a witch's claws." Give them some time to explore this before moving on to a new situation (like discovering the Gingerbread Cottage) or adding another character with words like, "You meet someone—who is it? Friend or foe? Find another actor and respond to one another. Will you move on together or will you avoid each other?"

This improvisation might also be done by starting with only two or three actors, adding others (such as the parents, a witch, a huntsman, or even a character from another story) as a scene develops.

For any age group, acting out a classroom scene will provide a familiar situation for testing acting ability. Ask for a volunteer to play the teacher, or perhaps the principal or another teacher. Tell the students to choose a character, i.e., class clown, shy violet, know-it-all, apple polisher, etc., or have these written on slips of paper ahead of time and let each actor draw one. Provide some conflict: the teacher is a substitute! Not only that, but her house burned down last week, and she is desperate for a permanent teaching position. Give a few of the students some conflict unbeknownst to the others: shy violet has a crush on the apple polisher, the know-it-all hates the apple polisher, the apple polisher is nervous about the class clown's pranks, etc. Then sit back and watch the scene develop. Notice who takes charge, which character says little or nothing, how the actors relate to one another, who is creative or inventive, who moves gracefully, is easily heard, and especially, seems to embody the qualities of the characters in your skit. Don't hesitate to help the action along by sending in the principal or another teacher with a message (play the part yourself if need be), or by interrupting with a fire drill or an announcement from the office over the intercom. If you think you haven't seen enough from a particular actor, have everyone switch roles and keep going, or try a new setting such as the shopping mall or the library.

Remember that you are looking for a combination of appearance, imagination, dramatic ability, and a voice and personality which will carry across the size of your performance space. You may discover that using students brings a lively enthusiasm to your library skit, but their relative inexperience requires more nurturing and more rehearsing. The student audience will readily respond to seeing their peers on stage, but your student actors may find it more difficult to control the audience, especially in some of the livelier scenes.

Working with adults as actors

I wouldn't recommend auditions if you decide to work with adult actors, simply because in most cases you will also be playing a part and the other actor is likely to be doing you a favor by helping out. Instead, think of the characters in your skit and the people who might be willing to work with you. Start at the top of your list of favorite choices and work your way down. Usually, I offer my fellow actor his/her choice of roles as a courtesy. People tend to pick a character somewhat like themselves in this case, so you may be able to guess ahead of time which role your helper will prefer!

On the other hand, it's perfectly acceptable to ask someone to play a particular role: "I'm doing a skit to promote the library reading club and I need someone to play the rabbit. Would you be interested?" Be sure to have a copy of the script handy for your potential co-star to take home and peruse.

Another tip: The less experienced actor is usually more comfortable playing the "straight man" rather than the "clown." This is especially true when performance day jitters set in, since the role of the "clown" bears most of the comedic responsibility.

Your target audience

Hand in hand with choosing a skit is deciding who will be your audience. The same skit can be done for first grade or fifth grade, but not in the same way. You may decide to focus your "advertising" on only one segment of the potential reading club population. If you do, you'll probably want to choose the age group which is least likely to seek out membership on its own.

In a school setting, you will probably want to perform for all grade levels. A word of advice: Grouping several close grade levels together takes away some of the peer pressure and allows the older children to let go and enjoy the silliness. Trying to span too many levels, i.e., first grade with fifth grade, will have the opposite effect. Either the first graders will be bored and restless, or more likely, the fifth graders will find the experience babyish. It is important to keep a sense of innocence when performing for younger students, while those in grades four and above usually respond better to a performance which is slightly tongue-in-cheek. Even so, it must be believable. If you don't believe it, they won't, and if you mock your own performance you will be encouraging them to mock it with you. Think of what each age group is watching on television. What else are they talking about in class or at the library? This will give you a clue as to how to play the skit.

Where to perform

Public librarians may choose to take the skit to the local schools to promote your reading club to a wider audience. A letter to the principal and a phone call to the school librarian will promote your cause. If this is to promote a summer reading club, you might ask for ten to fifteen minutes before the annual awards assembly. Kids find it hard to concentrate on anything (or even to sit still) on the school's sports or field day, so try to avoid performing on this day if you can. Another possibility is to perform the skit in the school library for one or two classes at a time. This is usually easy to arrange, but time your request well in advance since many school libraries close for inventory before the end of the school year. Performing for just a few classes at a time will also require more of your time.

It's best to choose a week or two and do all of your performances in that time period. You might suggest this time period in your letter, yet be willing to adapt to a more convenient time for a particular school. A sample letter can be found in appendix A.

Public librarians might choose to do a skit just before opening registration for the reading club. This adds a bit of splash to your opening day, and may draw a larger audience for the registration.

School librarians will most likely perform the skit within the school community. Consider having older students travel to another school in the district to perform for younger ones. This can be an exciting experience for both groups.

Teachers might direct their own students in a skit and perform it for another class in the building.

Many communities have a local cable television station, or at the very least a show which features community activities. Why not try to get the cable station to tape your performance for broadcast? They may be able to feature it during the nightly news broadcast even if they aren't able to present the entire skit during a regularly scheduled program.

Checklist

✔ Choose and adapt a skit to promote your reading club.

✔ Decide whether adults or students will perform.

✔ Hold auditions or ask colleagues to perform.

✔ Define your target audience.

✔ Contact performance sites to set dates for the skit.

✔ Set up a rehearsal schedule.

2
Rehearsals

The first rehearsal

Your cast is ready and it's time for the first rehearsal. What do you do?

Read the entire skit aloud together before trying to stage anything. This will give you both a feeling for the skit itself and a sense of how the other actor interprets his or her role. It also gives you a chance to discuss relevant sections before getting on your feet to move around.

The stage

Determine what your stage area will be like. Will you perform on a proscenium stage? This is the traditional stage, where the action of the play is framed as if it were a picture. Most schools have this type of stage in their auditorium, and this often presents the best sight line for your audience.

You may choose to perform in a flat space with your audience on the floor in front of you. Another option is to perform in the round, with the audience seated all around your playing area. Performing in the round is the most difficult way to stage a play, since you must be careful to face each side at one time or another. Any sight gag must be extended long enough to let all sides see the "punch line." Think of the clowns who walk around the circus ring repeating any joke which consists of a sight gag so that everyone will see it. It usually takes an experienced actor to work the audience successfully in such a situation, since the timing of any comic moments may be harder to pull off.

A good compromise to performing in the round is to seat the audience only around three-quarters of the circle. Not only does this eliminate the need to turn your body frequently or extend a joke, it also reduces the risk of stepping on a member of the audience when entering or exiting! This type of staging might work well if you are performing in the library itself.

Whatever type of stage you use, the most important thing to remember is that the actors must be seen and heard by the audience at all times when they are on stage.

Take the stage

After you've read through the play together and discussed the location of your stage areas, it is time to "take the stage." Walk through the skit as you read it aloud. Repeat this several times, allowing time for discussion in between. Don't try to perform any complicated actions just yet. Try to get a flow for the language and respond to each other's dialogue. Simple gestures will suffice at this point.

It isn't a good idea to memorize the script before the first rehearsal. This usually leads to a wooden, preset performance which loses the spontaneity of responding to a real live person—your fellow actor. The first rehearsal is a chance to get to know each other on stage, a chance to see and react to the life that another human being brings to a character.

After walking through the script several times, set up another rehearsal. It is best to schedule short, frequent rehearsals rather than long, infrequent ones. This will make it easier to learn the script. How many rehearsals will you need? That depends in part on how much time you can spare from other responsibilities and how comfortable you are with the performing process. At the very least, schedule three rehearsals. Plan for about 30 to 45 minutes for each rehearsal when you are doing a 10- to 15-minute skit. Arrange to have the most important props (or reasonable facsimiles) available at the second rehearsal and to become as familiar as possible with the script, though it isn't necessary to memorize it yet.

To memorize or not?

Another decision you will need to make early in the rehearsal schedule is whether you will perform with scripts in hand or memorize your lines. Actually, some learning of lines is required even if you will use scripts on stage, for you should know your dialogue well enough to be able to deliver your lines without reading word-for-word from the page.

Your decision may depend on the skit you choose. For example, in *Station W-Library*, the characters are radio broadcasters who have scripts in front of them. You can easily use your own script for the prop. *Trouble With Magic* would be difficult to perform if the lines are not memorized, since magic tricks and lots of action are involved.

An easy way to memorize your lines is to read through the script on your own several times a day. If you do this, you'll find that you are very familiar with your lines and cues by the time you rehearse again, but don't feel you have to leave your script off-stage just yet. It's more important to use the next rehearsal or two to explore your character now that you are familiar with the dialogue. Use this time to play with your character and with the other actor, to experiment with the timing and delivery of lines, to try out any ideas you think will add humor to the performance. *Have fun with each other!*

If you decide to use scripts during the performance, either because of nerves or too short a rehearsal period, it is important to keep that element of play and experimentation in the early rehearsal period. You will also be juggling with the script, for if you will be using it during the performance its use must be synchronized so that it doesn't get in the way. You will need to know exactly when you are holding the script and when and where you put it down, and then when you can pick it up again. Don't let the page turn get in the way. Ideally, the audience should *know* you are using the script, but never really *notice* you using it. You should be "acting," that is, speaking your lines in character, with meaning and expression and appropriate gestures and movement, and not merely reading the script.

Cheat sheets

There are ways to hide cue sheets among the props so that even if you are not using scripts on stage you won't get stuck if your mind suddenly goes blank. In *Reading Pleasures, Deep Sea Treasures*, the pirates can tape key words or lines on or in the treasure chest, or in one or two of the books inside the chest. A "cheat sheet" can be placed on the table next to the magician's hat in the magic skit, or next to the mixing bowl in the clown skit. In essence, you have permission to do anything you wouldn't want students to do during final exams! Just don't let the audience see you do it. You can use the props to cue you as well, by lining them up in the order you will use them.

In summary, the more comfortable you are with your lines, the more freedom you will have to play with your characterization, and the more fun you will have once the audience responds to your words and actions.

Staging the skit

At some point during the rehearsal period you will make decisions about props, costumes, and scenery. Each of the skits in this book has suggestions on how to find or make these with as little fuss as possible, but of course you are free to create your dramatization in any way you wish.

Scenery

Kids are quite ready to suspend belief, so it isn't necessary to have elaborate sets. A closed stage curtain will suffice, with the skit taking place in front of it. A large poster or sign placed on an easel to one side of the stage can let the audience know the setting, i.e., "A Deserted Beach Late at Night" for the pirate skit.

While keeping scenery simple or nonexistent is fine, be sure that any background which isn't part of the set doesn't distract the audience. We've arrived at some schools for a performance only to find the stage cluttered with chairs and music stands or with gym equipment. In that case, close the curtain and perform in front of it. The audience can readily imagine a deserted beach at midnight when the background is plain, but may have trouble forgetting about the upcoming spring concert with all those music stands about. If you are artistic, you may want to paint a few large paper trees or sand dunes, or whatever would be appropriate, but unless they are of good quality it is best to do without. Perhaps the art teacher or some art students will oblige you by helping out. Keep it simple, large, and colorful.

Props

Stage properties, or props, are any objects used on the stage. Props should also be large and colorful. Exaggeration adds humor: it's funnier to see an oversized mixing bowl with a giant spoon if two clowns are mixing the cake. Naturally, oversized props won't always be appropriate, but have fun with the props. The sillier they are, the more the audience will like it.

Don't limit yourself to what is asked for in the script; you may have better things available. In the clown skit, for example, Chlorine Clown puts some unusual things into the cake batter, among them a spider and a rat. You may have the perfect rubber snake for this occasion. *Go for it!* Substitute the snake for something else. The type of rubber chicken sold in magic stores would also be funny. Take a walk through your house with the eyes of the "Stage." You'll see things in a new light.

If you do use normal-sized props, be sure that your audience can see them. You might have to scrounge around for larger-than-life objects if you don't think they will be seen effectively from the back of a large auditorium. Remember to think *BIG*. A dinner fork may be too small to be seen from the back of the gym, but a pitchfork is perfect. Imagine Big Anthony eating all of Strega Nona's spaghetti with a pitchfork! Props can be cut out of oaktag and painted to look like the real thing. Don't worry about using real food items unless they will be eaten on stage. Use opaque containers so the audience won't know. If something must be dumped or poured, do it in such a way that the audience won't see the substance, i.e., lower the salt box into the bowl to pour. They'll never know the difference because, again, they are ready to suspend belief as long as you don't blatantly remind them of reality. You'll note one exception to this policy if you read the clown skit: Chlorine Clown pours real water from a glass dipped into a bucket. This is necessary to set up a special effect at the close of the skit, when the bucket is emptied onto the first row of the audience, who now expects to get soaked. Instead, they get confetti!

Costumes

Costumes should be comfortable. You should feel able to move freely. Avoid constricting seams which inhibit movement, and secure all pieces which might fall off.

Exaggerate color for good effect on the stage. The clowns needn't wear clown suits if they wear colorful shorts, pants, or skirts with mismatched tops and crazy hats or hairdos. The more color, the better.

Animal characters don't have to wear furry suits, which may be unavailable to you and would certainly be uncomfortable during a May or June performance. Each skit is followed by specific suggestions for costuming the characters, but in general, a plain running suit or just clothing in the appropriate color for that animal will do fine. A tail can be pinned on securely if you like, and ears can be made of paper or felt and attached to a headband. A little makeup on the nose or one of those vinyl animal noses which were popular in recent years will complete the illusion.

The final rehearsal

Plan to have a full dress rehearsal with the props you will use during the performance. This will give you a chance to iron out the kinks which will occur, to discover which pieces will fall off the costume or get in the way, which props are awkward, etc. It will give you a chance to adjust the stage business if necessary. You'll also find it lots of fun as everything comes together and you create a new reality on the stage. You'll be able to approach the first performance with excitement and confidence (except for those few butterflies which even professional actors experience).

Be sure that your final rehearsal is exactly as you plan to perform. If you won't be using your script on stage, don't use it at this rehearsal. If you forget a line or some stage business (stage movement, props, etc.), keep going and stay in character. Invite someone who works with you to sit in on this rehearsal or round up a few library patrons to watch if you aren't used to performing in front of an audience.

In many places, you will need to use a microphone in order to be heard. Practice with it at the final dress rehearsal if possible, because it will change your performance in some ways. Wireless mikes which can be worn on your clothing are best, but are usually not available in schools or libraries. Most schools do have a hand-held mike which can be attached to a stand. Trying to pass the mike back and forth slows the pace and gets confusing, so use the mike stand unless two mikes are available and you can each hold your own mike throughout the skit. The cords must be long enough to allow for entrances and exits, or you will have to work in when and where to pick up the mike.

Never put the mike down when the switch is in the "on" position, because it will make horrendous clunking sounds which will distract the audience. Also, be sure you don't carry the mike too close to a speaker. You'll know that you've done this when you hear a high-pitched squeal. Holding a mike in one hand will inhibit your use of props, so if you plan to do this, rehearse with a substitute until you use the real mike.

The easier solution is to put the microphone in its stand at center stage. Both actors will need to be aware of exactly how close to get to the mike in order to be heard, and this may vary with different microphones. If you are sharing a mike, you may need to lean in a bit to speak your dialogue and give way to your fellow actor when he/she is speaking.

Don't shy away from the idea of using a microphone. It's better to inhibit movement a bit and be heard by all.

You won't get your message across if the audience past the first three rows can't hear you. Try it; you'll get used to it. Since we use a microphone on a stand at center stage, most of the action in these skits stays near the mike. This will make it easier for you to adapt your own skit around a mike. In most cases, you'll probably discover that your voice will be picked up at a comfortable distance from the microphone.

Checklist

✔ Read through the play aloud together.

✔ Determine what your stage area will be like.

✔ Walk through the play as you read it aloud again.

✔ Don't memorize the script too soon.

✔ Schedule three or more 30-minute rehearsals.

✔ Learn your lines by reading them every day.

✔ Have fun during rehearsals!

✔ Keep scenery, if any, simple, large, and colorful.

✔ Use exaggerated props for humor.

✔ Be sure costumes are easy to move in.

✔ Create cheat sheets if you need them.

✔ Have a full dress rehearsal.

✔ Plan to use a microphone if necessary.

3
Acting: Quick Study for the Novice

It may be that you've never set foot on a stage. You still have natural talents and life experience from which to draw. This chapter gives you tips on how to polish your act.

Stay in character

The actor's objective is always to communicate. It isn't enough to communicate the author's lines of dialogue. Dialogue serves as a tool for the thoughts and feelings of the character, which are expressed by actions—or by lack of action. Every word, every movement on stage portrays the character. Thus it is important to stay in character even when your character isn't speaking. As an actor, you must listen "in character" to the other actors. Picture someone at a party, sitting bored and lifeless until he is able to make a comment; when he speaks, his eyes sparkle, his body straightens with new energy which seems to extend beyond the limits of mere flesh, his voice conveys feeling and passion for the topic of conversation. Then, when he finishes speaking and someone else chimes in, he once more sits bored and lifeless, just waiting for his turn again.

This is not something you would see in real life, and except in a comedy routine which exaggerates for some other purpose, you don't want to see it on the stage. Everything the actor does while on stage must be done the way the character that he/she portrays would do it. From the entrance until the final exit, every move and gesture, even the way the actor stands, must express the character in the play. It's no wonder so many directors rely on type casting.

The entrance

Let's look at the entrance of a character, for example. In most cases, when performing the skits in this book, your character will need to make an entrance in order to get to the main playing area of your stage. You can't just walk out as Anne the librarian or Tom the teacher and then "turn on" the rabbit or the pirate character as if someone had flipped a switch. Doing that will also rob the audience of a chance to get to know your character right away. In the circus skit, Chlorine Clown is upset when she enters because the ringmaster has left her in the lurch. As an actor, you might choose to stomp on in a huff, stopping to crack the whip every few steps. Or you might choose to enter with short, quick steps and jump in frustration when you crack the whip. Either will work, as will other choices, so it is up to you as actor to decide whether you want to emphasize Chlorine's anger or her frustration.

Whichever you choose, remember that emotions on stage are shown by action. It isn't enough to rely on facial expressions. You must do something which will show how your character feels. A well-known expression in the theater is "Show, don't tell." How do you know what to do? Just answer this question: What does my character want?

The objective

As an actor, you will need to comb the script to find out what your character wants in each moment. Sometimes that will stay the same for a while and sometimes it may change because of the action or dialogue of other characters.

"What the character wants" is considered his/her goal or objective, and there are usually two going on at the same time: an immediate objective and an overall objective.

For example, the overall objective for Pocus Hocus in *Trouble With Magic* is to entertain the audience. No matter what, she is determined to do this. Usually this entails setting up the stage and assisting the Great Presto Chango, but when the skit is taking place, there has been a mix-up in the time. Nevertheless, the children must be entertained, so her immediate objective is to perform some tricks. This immediate objective changes as each trick backfires, which leads to the objective of getting the rabbit back in the hat—and this ultimately sends her to the library (which is *your* objective in performing the skit).

Each actor in the skit must answer the question, "What does my character want?" The answer can be found in the script. Once you know what your character wants, keep it in mind, even when listening to the other characters. In *Station W-Library*, there are times when Bear can barely keep quiet because he is so irritated with Hare. Bear cannot be a passive listener. Instead, he must let that irritation ooze from every pore without saying a word until his next line. Think of Jackie Gleason playing Ralph Cramden in The Honeymooners, exasperated time and again with his neighbor, Ed Norton.

Comedy and timing

It helps to have a visual image of your character, and it is perfectly acceptable to use people you know either in real life or in the entertainment world. The skits in this book use two actors in classic comedic style: one character is the clown and the other the straight man. Both roles are funny. Think of Jackie Gleason and Art Carney, Abbott and Costello, Laurel and Hardy, Lucille Ball and any of her co-actors. There are times when we laugh at the antics of the "clown" in the pair, but we also laugh at the reaction of the "straight man." All of the actors mentioned above are masters of comedic timing.

What is timing? Timing is what makes comedy work. It is difficult to teach, especially in a book, for it relies on developing a feel for the rhythm of a piece. It involves delayed reactions when appropriate, and holding just long enough for the audience to laugh at a joke without letting the laugh die down. Timing is a delicate art, for if the actor doesn't wait long enough during an audience's response, the audience doesn't hear the next line. If you are on stage and this happens to you, just repeat the line as soon as you feel the audience is ready. Performing for a live audience is like having another character on the stage, particularly in skits like these, which invite audience participation.

It is important to keep the pace going in comedy. The interrupted rhythm will act as a laugh magnet. Timing happens in coordination with another actor, like a well-choreographed dance. A sudden change in the pace of the dialogue by one character, or an unexpected change in voice or movement will bring a laugh, but the balance is precarious. If one tries too hard it isn't funny anymore. Simplicity is important. Trying too hard will create a busy scene which will spread the audience's attention rather than focus it.

Are you ready to give up? Don't despair! The key to timing is listening to what other people are saying and doing on the stage (and this includes that other character, the audience). By listening, you will develop a feel for the pattern of the dialogue. Pay attention to the author's punctuation and stage directions, for this will also help you "hear" what is going on. Now that you are aware of some of the elements of comedic timing, watch a few episodes of any sitcom on television. You can learn a lot, especially from the great talents like Gleason, Carney, and Ball, once you know what to look for. If their broad humor isn't your cup of tea, try some of the British comedies often shown on public television stations. Even though television programs are not usually filmed with a live audience, the elements of comedic timing are there and you will be able to pick up some tips. You'll discover things that work and things which you think don't work, and you will find your personal level of comfort in comedy. Not everyone wants to perform the incredibly zany antics of Lucille Ball, and that's perfectly acceptable.

One more note about laughter: pause while the audience laughs, but don't wait until it ends before continuing with the next line. Think of laughter as a wave rolling in to shore: it builds slowly, and when it reaches its crest it thunders on top of itself before flattening out on the beach and rolling back to sea. Go on with the next line when the wave just hits the beach. Don't wait for it to flatten out completely or roll back to the sea.

Movement

Unless you are performing in a small library setting, your audience for most of these skits will be large. Movement on stage must be exaggerated for a large audience. Yet exaggerated movement is easy to overdo. Let common sense be your guide. Let's say, for example, that your character is directed to put out his hand, palm up, in a gesture which is saying to your fellow actor and to the audience, "Give it to me right here." In real life or in a small theater space it is usually enough to gently lift the hand, palm upwards, and pause. For the most part, the hand, the wrist, and the forearm will be involved in this movement. In a large space, such as a school cafeteria or auditorium, such a small gesture will be lost at the "back of the house," the last few rows of the auditorium. In this space, it would be better to involve the whole arm in the movement. It needn't be overemphasized or made into a big production—that would be overexaggerating. Perform the move just as simply, but with the whole arm, not just the forearm. If you put your whole body into it, i.e., stamping your foot, jiggling impatiently, and making faces, you are probably overacting. Use your common sense. If it feels right, it probably is right, and if you aren't sure, ask someone (even your fellow actor) for his/her opinion.

Energy makes a gesture exciting or dull. Try the movement of the hand described in the previous paragraph. When you have done that, try it again, but this time feel the energy extend beyond your fingers in a direct line to the other actor. On the stage, movement never ends with the physical boundaries of our bodies. Each movement must extend beyond the body into the surrounding space. This will become second nature to you in time, so don't worry about it every minute on stage, but do think about it while rehearsing, especially during any important movements on stage. Again, let common sense guide you. In the end, it will make the difference between a dull performance and one which crackles with life.

What to move when

Hundreds of years later, Hamlet's advice to the Players still rings true: "Suit the words to the action, the action to the words." The common sense approach to theater asks merely that the actions be appropriate to your character at that moment, and that there not be so many actions that they detract from the scene.

One of the biggest mistakes beginning actors make is not standing still. Someone who isn't used to speaking in front of an audience, whether to give a speech, sing a song, act in a play, or tell a story often paces restlessly while talking. By now you probably have an image of Groucho Marx pacing from wall to wall, chomping on a cigar, and you may be thinking, "I've never seen anyone do that." The nervous speaker doesn't usually go to such extremes, but instead has a hard time keeping his feet planted. There is something about trying to reach an audience which compels us to unconsciously move our feet. It is usually a subtle lifting and replacing in not quite the same spot. One of the first things beginning actors learn is to stand still when it is time to stand still and to walk when it is time to walk. This adds strength to any performance and eliminates the effect of uncertain hedging motions. There must be a reason for every movement on the stage, even if the audience doesn't know that reason.

Many times an actor moves to facilitate a later movement. For example, it may be too awkward to cross from right center to left center (see appendix B for a diagram of the stage areas) and pick up a prop in time to say "Here it is!" If doing this throws off the timing or interrupts the flow of the dialogue, the actor must make a preliminary cross. The real motivation is to make the next move easier, but the character must still have a reason for moving, such as "I want to get away from that other character" or "I'm hungry and there is some pie in the kitchen" or even the classic "I have to go to the bathroom." The audience won't know your motivation, and won't care—as long as the move looks natural. Note that the motivation isn't necessarily completed: If your character really left to eat that pie in the kitchen, he/she wouldn't be on stage to say, "Here it is!" When you have a reason for moving, it eliminates aimless wandering. Since you aren't really leaving the stage at this time, another motivation interrupts this first one and becomes more important, leaving you just where you need to be for that next line.

The same is true for entrances and exits: Your character has just come from somewhere when entering the scene, and you, as actor, should know where and why. The answer can usually be found in the script. When you leave the stage, your character is going somewhere for a purpose. For example, when Cotton Candy Clown exits right, she is going to announce the next circus act. When the pirates enter left, they have just come from the ship. In fact, their destination is off-stage, in search of a viable spot for burying treasure. This is also an example of movement which is interrupted: Flotsam is too tired to continue.

There is an exception to every rule, and the exception to this one is the "countercross." If Actor A is speaking and moving from right to left, Actor B may counter or balance that move by moving from left to right at the same time. The audience's attention is focused on Actor A, who is speaking while moving. The audience won't pay attention to Actor B, who is quiet. Such a cross should be simple and unobtrusive. It is usually done to avoid clumping actors together or to free Actor B for his next move. Sometimes it is done simply because there isn't enough room for both actors to stand at that spot. Actor B is getting out of Actor A's way. Being the dominant actor at that moment, Actor A gets the downstage cross. If Actor B were to cross in front of Actor A, it would call attention to the countercross. In other words, the actor who is speaking crosses nearest the audience. The audience will focus on that actor and not even notice the other one moving upstage. When making any cross, the shortest route is usually the best. Avoid backing up, unless there is a reason for the character to do this. In most cases, backing up is a weak move, and an unrealistic one. Instead, just turn and move off at the appropriate time.

Quick tips

- Face the audience or stand with three-quarters of your body facing the audience as much as possible. This is called "cheating," and every actor must do it to pass muster on the stage. We all know you are speaking to the other character, but if you really face the other character we, as audience, can't see and hear you. It feels funny at first, but do it anyway; you'll get used to it.

- When you turn, whether in handling a prop, relating to another actor, or to make a cross, always turn toward the audience. This is an open turn, and allows the audience to see and hear you.

- Always use your upstage hand (the one furthest from the audience) when reaching out to another actor or handling a prop. Again, this keeps your body open so that the audience can see you. Using the downstage hand puts your body in profile, hiding your face. The same is true of your feet when making a cross or taking a few steps.

- Avoid eye contact with the audience unless you are speaking or reacting directly to them. Audience participation is used in these skits, and when appropriate you will need to direct your actions to them, but for the most part, direct your lines to the back wall of the auditorium.

- Articulate your lines when you speak. Be careful not to rush words (particularly those of multiple syllables) or to swallow endings by unconsciously lowering your voice at the ends of sentences. Do each other a service by pointing out anything of this sort, since we often can't tell when we are doing this.

- Only use an accent or funny voice for your character if you can sustain it throughout the entire skit.

- The character with the last line will exit last, even though you may be going out together.

- To keep the skit moving smoothly, pick up the cues. There is a rhythm to the speech and action, and waiting too long to speak the next line or perform a gesture will distort the rhythm. If the skit drags, you will lose your audience. As you probably know, children have no patience with a dull performance. Picking up the cues doesn't mean speaking the entire line faster. Just begin your line when the other character finishes speaking. Keep the rhythm going. A dramatic pause can be funny if it breaks the rhythm for just a moment.

- If something goes wrong during the performance, stay in character and keep going. The audience won't know that you've made a mistake unless you give it away by stopping or losing the rhythm. If you forget a line, your fellow actor is often able to help you out by incorporating your line into his. If you forget something important to the plot, try to work it in as soon as you can. Again, your fellow actor will help. Often, when learning lines, actors naturally learn the lines of other characters, since these are cue lines for them. Above all, stay in character.

- If you discover that you are nervous before starting the performance, don't despair! You are in good company. All actors are nervous before performing, and every actor has had "the actor's nightmare," a dream in which he/she is performing an important role before thousands of people—and can't remember a single line! If you find your mind going blank as the audience files into the auditorium, just run over your first few lines in your head as you stand backstage. It's okay to look at your script while you wait, but just look at the first page and any especially troublesome spots. Once you get going on stage, if you are well-rehearsed, the rhythm will carry you, and everything will fall into place.

4
Writing Your Own Skits

Theater is creative, and creativity is fun. Keep this in mind as you develop your own script for a reading club skit, and have fun with it.

Starting off

Before you can begin to write your own skit, you must choose the theme of your reading club. Then you can begin your research. I was fortunate enough to come across a book of sea slang which inspired the pirate skit, but most of the time more extended research is needed. Why bother? Because research will give you a treasure house of ideas to work with rather than a mere closetful.

Usually I have my characters in mind as I begin the research, and if not, I discover them quickly. The setting may be more difficult. Sometimes the reading club theme itself provides the obvious setting, such as the circus, but even then one needs to know where in the circus the action will take place. Circumstances may simplify this decision process: I knew I didn't want three rings of circus acts on the school stage! That, to me, would be too much work to write and perform, require more people than I had available, and would ultimately detract from my purpose: to promote the reading club.

Research: Making lists

It isn't necessary to write lengthy paragraphs when doing your research. Instead, jot down words; phrases; ideas; characters; names of people, places, and things; historical data—anything, in short, that captures your fancy.

Don't overlook joke books! You may find great one-liners there, as well as classic joke situations which you may be able to adapt to your purpose.

Brainstorm with other people. Talk about the topic, play with words and ideas, get silly! Keep your pad and pencil handy, and add these things to your list.

Here is an early list from the circus skit, composed while leafing through heavily illustrated books:

Circus terms
circus band
ringmaster
acrobats
jugglers
high wire walkers
clowns
animals & trainers
side show
one ring/three ring
colorful costumes/sequins
gold & silver thread
cloaks/tights/big shoes
brightly colored pants
striped socks
wigs/chiffon scarves/makeup

Props
tent poles
strong wooden boxes
rope
bicycles/unicycle
skateboards/hoops
balloons/pennants
flowers

Circus parade
kazoos/drums
animals/performers
tin can stilts
strong man

Food
popcorn/peanuts
cotton candy
hot dogs
ice cream
soda

At this point, I knew at least one of my characters would be a clown, but in listing what I saw in the books, I was toying with ideas for the other character. Your skit can have as many characters as you want. I limit mine to two characters because it makes scheduling performances and covering the reference desk easier at our library.

As my research continued, I discovered a book of clown techniques, and decided that both characters should be clowns. In the end, I had approximately six to eight pages of lists. This later sampling includes snatches of dialogue:

Circus jokes
Big Top
Why did the clown cross the road?
Knock knock!
peanut butter and jellyfish sandwich
gorilla cheese sandwich
Ring! (Discovery—pick up French bread)
   "Hello? Sorry, wrong number!"
Ring! (Discovery—pick up mixing spoon)
   "Hello? Sorry, wrong number!"
Ring! (Discovery—pick up own shoe)
   "Sorry, the lion is busy. Would you care to talk to the seal?"
lion's share
put the kettle on (tries to wear it)
sharp as a tack ("Yeah, you are a little tacky")
monkey business
sealed with a kiss
Flea: "Help me! I've fallen and I can't get up!"

As you can see if you take a look at the circus skit, most of this didn't make it into the final script. During the research/brainstorming process, I don't know what will be most useful. When I discovered the classic phone joke, I twisted it to suit what I had learned from another part of my research: "Discovery" is a traditional clown reaction, in which the clown searches for the source of (in this case) the ringing. Finding no telephone, he "discovers" that the bread is ringing, and answers it as if that were the normal thing to do. There were two reasons for leaving it out of the final script: The skit was getting too long, and I didn't want to search for or create a ringing sound effect.

Something else which is always a part of my lists is word play. Take a phrase like "monkey business" and jot down anything that comes to mind using the word "monkey." My list included:

monkeyshines
monkey around,
make a monkey out of me
monkey wrench

The phrase "big top" led to:

big deal
big shot
big time
big cheese
big wheel
top dog
top banana
tip top
big ticket
big talk
the big one

Combining my two original phrases leads to "big business!" How would I use this? Character A might say something about entering the big top, the main circus tent, for the next act. Character B can say something like, "We're doing big business tonight," to which Character

A responds, "It'll be monkey business if you don't get on with the show!"

When I find a word or phrase which yields a lot of possibilities—or even one that I like a lot—I consult a rhyming dictionary, a dictionary of slang, and a dictionary of phrases. This both clarifies the meaning of the word or phrase and also leads to new ones. During the actual writing process, I go back to my lists for material for jokes and snappy dialogue.

The outline

A string of jokes and one-liners doesn't make a skit. At this point, you have information about the reading program and lists of words and phrases, with maybe a bit of dialogue and background information mixed in. You need a story. For now, a short annotation is enough, i.e., "Pocus Hocus, a magician's assistant, is getting ready for a magic show at the school when she discovers that the audience is already present." There is a main character, a setting, and a problem. This is enough to begin with, but answer a few more questions before you do.

Why is the audience present? Are they early or is Pocus Hocus late? Why? What is Pocus Hocus going to do to solve the problem? Will that work? Why or why not? What next?

Continue asking and answering these questions until the story has developed to a point where the characters can get information about the library and make plans to go there. Bring in as many characters as you want to add to the dilemma or provide attempts at a solution. In *Trouble With Magic*, Pocus Hocus has made a scheduling error, and the magician will be late, so she cashes in on her dream of being the star by performing a few tricks herself. When she tries to pull a rabbit out of the magic hat, the trick backfires, and she is stuck with a giant rabbit who won't fit in the hat. Her objective changes from "I want to entertain the children" to "I have to get this rabbit back in the hat before the Great Presto Chango discovers what I've done."

After repeated failures, the rabbit finds a reading club announcement from the local library. This leads the frustrated pair to try the library for a solution to their problem—and, naturally, they join the reading club while they are there! If the plot is reminiscent of "The Sorcerer's Apprentice," I assure you that it wasn't a conscious decision. It is perfectly acceptable to borrow plot complications from classic literature, and even from shows and movies. An idea cannot be copyrighted. What you do with the idea will be different from what someone else does with the same idea. Using the same characters or some actual dialogue, however, is stealing.

The hook

It helps to have a "hook" on which to hang your plot. In *Trouble With Magic*, the hook is magic. Magic is the theme, and magic is what goes wrong. Everything in the plot revolves around that. In *Three-Ring Reading*, the hook is mixing the cake. No matter what else the two clowns are doing, they always come back to that cake. In the pirate skit, the hook is simply the treasure chest itself.

The hook will help you get from point A to point B to point C in your story, picking up jokes and information (the message you are sending with this "commercial") along the way. It may be an interrupted task, such as mixing the cake, or it may be an "interrupting" task, such as answering a phone which keeps ringing. It may be a prop or a character (such as Turtle in *Station W-Library*, who never actually appears on the stage). Whatever it is, it must be important to the characters.

When the plot complications develop, they will develop around the hook, either directly or indirectly. The pirates Flotsam and Jetsam can't find the map needed to bury the treasure chest. Hocus Pocus's magic trick backfires and she can't get the rabbit back in the hat. Chlorine and Cotton Candy Clown keep adding "improvements" to their cake batter. The hook will provide material for humorous dialogue and funny situations.

Where to find ideas

The story line and key plot incidents may come from classic literature, but for other details you may be able to draw on your personal experiences. With your theme and characters in mind, think back to the most embarrassing thing that ever happened to you, or the time when you really goofed, or perhaps when you got the biggest surprise in your life. A frightening experience may lead to a spooky situation for your characters.

The hook for the clown skit came out of an unfinished short story I'd written nearly ten years ago. Thinking of the characters and what they could do led me to thinking about surprises, since clowns are usually full of them, which led me to a surprise party at which they would need—a cake! I played "What if...?" with my old story, "Marvin's Marvelous Meatballs," in which various family members add their favorite ingredient to the meat mixture behind Marvin's back. What if the "meatballs" were a birthday cake? What if the clowns added zany ingredients themselves? I started with literal mistakes, like "flower" for "flour," and tasting the sugar instead of adding enough to suit one's personal taste. A little research into classic clown characteristics and some well-known clown routines made me realize that I had my hook.

Trying to use a sports/Olympics theme with only two characters had me wrestling with a number of ideas before I hit upon the solution, which came from my own life. A friend was working in radio, which led me to the idea of sports broadcasting. My research in this case focused on radio and the Olympics. I had enjoyed the rabbit character from *Trouble With Magic*, so I renamed him Hare and paired him with a burly Bear, since I found the rhyme funny. Hare stuck to his usual tricks and shenanigans while Bear played the straight man.

You may get ideas from history. Dinosaurs and Egyptology are perennial favorites with kids. Would your theme be appropriate in such a setting? Classic literature may also provide a story line. What if your characters went through the looking glass? Take a story from folk literature, such as "The Three Wishes," and change it. What if, once the man has wished the sausage on his wife's nose, he won't waste his last wish by wishing it off again? What else could they do? You might modernize it by having them make a series of funny phone calls. The sausage would be the hook, for all the calls would concern how to remove it without using the wish. How does the wife feel about this? Does she want the man to use his wish to set her free? Is she willing to try other solutions first? What if he tried to eat her nose? Her response to the changing situation can add a lot of humor.

Eventually, they can call the library, learn about the reading program, and make their exit with immediate plans to join the reading club and earn prizes to compensate for the lost wishes (or, conversely, go to the library for more information on removing sausages from noses, with plans to join the reading club to while away the time as they wait for various solutions to take effect).

Character biographies

Writing a short history of each character is a helpful tool. As with the lists, not all of the information will work its way into the final script, but you may be surprised at what does. You may also be surprised at how the characters change as you write the script.

A short paragraph or two, or a page of phrases, descriptions, and characteristics is all you need for the character biography. If you would like to know where your character was born and what his/her parents were like, then go ahead and write that down. As with all aspects of writing your own skit, you should have fun. Play with ideas. If it's enough for you to know that Cotton Candy Clown was born in a trunk, then that's fine, too. Perhaps that explains why her brains are addled. If she were born in an elephant's trunk, it might explain why she has peanuts for brains, or why she works for circus peanuts.

Whatever the length of your character bio, be sure to answer key questions like "What do I want?" and "How do I feel about each of the other characters?" Don't forget to include characters who appear in the dialogue but never on the stage when you answer that last question. It isn't necessary to write a biography for the bearded lady, for instance, but both Chlorine Clown and Cotton Candy need to know how they feel about the bearded lady and what role she plays in their lives. Is she a close friend? Are they rivals? Making a cake for a rival can be a humorous situation. What if the bearded lady were new to the circus and the clowns were making a cake to welcome her? Why do they want to make a good impression on her? Or do they?

Chlorine became nicer as the skit developed, and nicer yet during performances, and that was fine. Initially, her biography states that she wants to be the boss, to tell others what to do, and to become either the ringmaster or the ringmaster's wife. That changed during the writing process, when I decided she couldn't tell Cotton Candy what to do and do it herself at the same time. At first, Chlorine was jealous of the bearded lady, but as the script developed she became more upset at the ringmaster for leaving the circus in the lurch. If this skit were to be performed for teenagers, I might have developed the jealousy angle and focused on a romance, but I felt that primary grade students wouldn't relate to that as well. Chlorine is possessive and likes to hold on to things. She is intelligent, pompous, proud, yet innocent and lovable—somewhat like a know-it-all five-year-old. She moves in a no-nonsense fashion. You might envision a character like Lucy in the *Peanuts* comic strips by Charles Schulz.

This was a very sketchy bio, yet it gave me enough of a feeling for Chlorine Clown to get started on the script. Remember that each character must have a motivating force, or objective, which will be found in answer to the question, "What do I want?" This force drives the character through the situation depicted on the stage, for every action or choice that character makes brings him/her closer (or so he thinks) to that objective.

The script

Begin at the beginning. Picture your character or characters as they first enter the playing area. It helps to visualize the unfolding action, as if watching a movie. How does your character walk? What is he/she doing here? What is the motivating force or objective? Your story outline and character bio will provide answers to these questions—and the skit begins.

What is the first thing that your character says? Remember that the audience gets their information about the setting and characters through the dialogue. It helps to have the characters address each other by name very early in the skit. If only one character is on stage to start, he/she might name the other character. ("It's the bearded lady's birthday, and Chlorine Clown and I are going to make her a cake!") It is also helpful to have the characters comment on the setting. ("It's so dark on this beach I can hardly see!" "Well, what did you expect at midnight?")

Once you've introduced the characters and setting, get to the problem as soon as you can. Here again, your outline will help.

When writing the dialogue, continue to see the picture develop in front of you, and listen to what each character is saying. As the characters converse, pin each line of dialogue on the one before it by either answering a question or using a key word or phrase in a different way in the new sentence. This technique will give you many opportunities for word play and one-line jokes.

Listen to the way people talk and adapt that to the stage. For example, although we are encouraged to write in complete sentences, people don't always speak in complete sentences. Use that trait when writing dialogue. This will help establish the rhythm and will also feel natural to both the actors and the audience. On the other hand, in real life people repeat a lot and interject things like "um" or "you know." On stage, this will break the rhythm and slow the action, resulting in a dull sketch instead of a lively, informative conversation. In most cases, avoid long speeches made by one character, at least while more than one character is on stage. (As an exception to the rule, that could be your "hook": One character can ramble on while the other constantly interrupts with the information you want the kids to hear!)

If you write a few pages and discover that it is taking too long to get to the action, try starting the skit later on in the sequence.

The ideal time for the skit to begin is just before the story problem develops. We don't want to see Flotsam and Jetsam leaving the rowboat which brought them ashore and stumbling down a long stretch of deserted beach before finally realizing that they don't have a map. Let the action begin just before they make this discovery. It is more effective when Chlorine Clown enters, cracking the ringmaster's whip, with the announcement that the ringmaster is missing and the show about to begin than it would be to follow her trail as she looks for him throughout the circus.

"Discovery" is a key word in beginning the script. Whatever the setting, whatever the problem, let the action begin just before the characters discover that problem. It can be as blatant as walking on stage expecting a certain situation to exist only to "discover" a note explaining the problem. For example, Chlorine Clown could have entered the stage expecting to see the ringmaster and instead have found a note explaining his whereabouts. The audience still has all it needs to know, but the "how" is different. There is always more than one way to go about it.

Adapting the skits

Feel free to change any of the skits in this book for your own performance. There are certain words or phrases which are underlined or in some cases left out. This is where you can personalize the skit for your own reading club, using your library's name and mentioning specific programs, people, or details. Don't bog down in details. The kids will remember your message, but not much more. Plan to give out brochures or flyers which highlight important dates or procedures. It's enough for the kids to remember that there is going to be a reading club, and it's going to be great, and they want to join! Put the rest of the information in their hands. Do give enough information to make the club sound exciting, like mentioning a ballet class or a treasure chest of prizes. Think of it as a teaser, which will leave them wanting more.

If you are working with students and want to add more parts, be creative! Let the circus parade march through the clowns' tent in the circus skit, or have various acts cross the stage. A whole gang of pirates can bury the treasure chest. Be ridiculous—what if the old woman who lived in a shoe popped into the skit with all of her children? What would happen, and how would that change things? You may find it easier to adapt one of these skits by writing a new scene than trying to write a whole new skit yourself. Whatever you do, *have fun with it*. You may not win the Pulitzer Prize for drama, but you will promote a positive image about books and libraries to children, and that in itself is an award.

5
Reading Pleasures, Deep Sea Treasures
By Anne Lemay

A skit for two players

Characters:

FLOTSAM, a pirate
JETSAM, his shipmate

Setting: A lonely beach on the east coast late at night.

At rise: *Two pirates,* Flotsam and Jetsam, *enter from left.* Jetsam *leads, carrying a lantern and a shovel.* Flotsam *follows, dragging a treasure chest by a rope, looking exhausted.*

FLOTSAM: *(puffing)* Hold on, mate. I can't go much further.

JETSAM: *(stops at center)* I *told* you not to have that extra drink.

FLOTSAM: Nah, it wasn't that. Milk makes you strong. *(Drops rope and crosses behind chest to push while singing)* "Yo-ho-ho and a bottle of milk!" *(collapses over treasure chest)*

JETSAM: *(nervous)* Shake a leg, Flotsam. If we don't have this chest buried by midnight, Captain Kidd will make us… *(stage whisper)* walk the plank.

FLOTSAM: *(shudders)* You mean…?

JETSAM: *(nods)* Then it's Davy Jones's Locker dead ahead.

FLOTSAM: *(moans)* Ooooh, I've heard some scary tales about that.

JETSAM: And you *don't* want to find out if they're true. *(Jetsam turns to walk away)*

FLOTSAM: Wait a minute, Jetsam! How is Captain Kidd gonna know where to find the chest?

JETSAM: From the map, Dead Head. You know, "X" marks the spot.

FLOTSAM: What map?

JETSAM: *(feels clothing and pockets for map)* Blimey! We forgot the map. We're dead meat now.

FLOTSAM: Maybe it's in the chest. Let's open it.

JETSAM: No way! There'll be the devil to pay if we do.

FLOTSAM: Then let's forget Captain Kidd. I never liked the cut of his jib anyhow. We'll keep the treasure for ourselves and set up as rich merchants.

JETSAM: *(thinks it over)* All right … but only if there is no map inside!

(Flotsam and Jetsam stand downstage of treasure chest and open it)

JETSAM: *(shouts)* Hey, this ain't no treasure! Just a bunch of books. *(begins to unload books from chest)*

FLOTSAM: *(picks up a scroll and unrolls it)* Well, I'll be a dog's body! Look at this. Captain Kidd was holding out on us. *(taps scroll)* This says "Kidd's Kapers." It's some kind of plan.

JETSAM: Why that old pirate! He didn't want us to know the ropes.

FLOTSAM: *(reads from scroll)* "Reading Pleasures, Deep Sea Treasures Reading Club."

Jetsam: *(looks over Flotsam's shoulder)* Hey! It's only for the kids in *(name of town here)*! Kidd was trying to cut us out.

Flotsam: And look at this list of books! Captain Kidd had all kinds of plans. Hey, Jetsam! *(jabs him with elbow)* There are books about ballet listed here.

Jetsam: *(pirouettes)* I don't need them. But I'd like to find some books about the songs of whales. *(takes scroll from Flotsam)*

Flotsam: I want to read *Rip Van Winkle*. It's about ghosts and a man who sleeps for 20 years. *(yawns)* I could use a good sleep.

Jetsam: Flotsam! Captain Kidd was planning to do us in. Look! There are tales from Davy Jones's Locker on this list. We'd better steer clear of them.

Flotsam: But that sounds first rate! I always like a good ghost story.

Jetsam: Even when the ghost is yours…? *(shows scroll to Flotsam)*

Flotsam: *(grimly)* You're right. Captain Kidd has shown his true colors at last. Let's lower the boom on him.

Jetsam: How?

Flotsam: Kidd must have pirated this treasure from some library, right?

Jetsam: Right.

Flotsam: If we bring it back, maybe they'll let us join the reading club.

Jetsam: They'd better. You can win prizes just by reading books.

Flotsam: There you go: Books *are* a treasure. And you don't even need a map—just a library card.

Jetsam: Yeah, and everybody knows a library card is free. Hey, let's go find the library now.

Flotsam: Nah, we can't. It's almost midnight. The library isn't open.

Jetsam: Then let's read some of these books in the treasure chest while we wait. *(chooses a book and sits, leaning back on chest)* I bet I can read more books than you.

Flotsam: *(choosing his book and sitting opposite Jetsam)* I bet I can read longer ones.

Jetsam: I bet I can remember the stories better than you can.

Flotsam: I bet you can't. *(sings)* "Sixteen books in a dead man's chest…"

Jetsam: *(joins in)* "…Yo-ho-ho and a bottle of milk!"

The End

Production Notes

Setting

The action takes place on a bare stage or before a closed curtain. If desired, a sign on an easel to one side may read "A lonely beach, late at night." If possible, emphasize the ending of the skit by enlisting someone ahead of time to close the curtain or turn off the lights. If this is not possible, the actors should hold their positions for a minute, then get up and take a bow or walk off the stage.

Costumes

Both pirates can wear knickers or baggy pants. If neither are available, baggy knickers can be made out of a long skirt: when the skirt is on the actor, draw the back hem up between the legs to the front, where it can be pinned from the inside front of the skirt.

Shirts can either be white with full sleeves or striped rugby shirts. Vests may be worn if desired. Use a long swatch of material tied around the waist for a sash. Another can be tied around the head as a kerchief, gypsy-style. Tie a bandana around the neck, and put a gold earring on one ear. Footwear can be black clunky shoes with gold buckles, knee-length boots, or bare feet.

Props

treasure chest
wagon (optional)
books
scroll
lantern
shovel
rope

Props Notes

If a real *chest* can be located, that is ideal. If not, improvise with a cardboard carton painted to look like a chest. The treasure chest may have wheels *(especially if it is a real trunk)*, or may be light enough to drag. A cardboard carton may be dragged without scratching the floor, but be careful if you are using a real chest. In that case, pulling the treasure chest on a *wagon* rather than by a rope will solve the problem.

The entire chest need not be filled with *books*. Instead, pile light blankets or empty boxes in the chest and put in just enough books to show when the cover is lifted and for the pirates to pull out and look at.

The *scroll* can be made out of shelf paper or by taping standard size sheets of paper together.

If a real *lantern* is not available *(any old-fashioned-looking tin or metal candle lantern will do)*, cut the sides of a half-gallon milk carton to look like the windows of a lantern, and paint it black. A metal ring or a piece of twine or rope will serve as a handle. If you would like the lantern to look as if it were lit, use a small flashlight or some shiny paper in red or gold inside the lantern.

The *shovel* should be large, preferably one designed for digging earth. Once again, if such a shovel is not available, improvise with a cardboard cutout painted appropriately or even, for a touch of humor, use a snow shovel!

Any *rope* will do to pull the treasure chest across the floor.

6
Trouble With Magic
By Anne Lemay

A skit for two players

Characters:

Pocus Hocus, a magician's assistant
Rabbit, from the magician's hat

Setting: *A stage in the school auditorium where the Great Presto Chango will be performing. There is a table at center, covered with a magician's cloth. A black magician's hat sits on top. A large poster on an easel announces the show at far right.*

At rise: *The stage is empty. Pocus Hocus rushes on stage from left carrying additional props for the show.*

Pocus Hocus: Oh, dear, oh, dear! I'm running late. I've got to set up these magic tricks before the Great Presto Chango arrives for the show. *(sees Audience)*

Abracadzooks! What are you doing here? You aren't here for the show! You are? But you're too early. Look here, the poster says "The Great Presto Chango presents Books Are Magic at (5:49)."* It's only (9:45). Are you sure you're supposed to be here now? Let me check the Great Presto Chango's schedule.

(pulls out a calendar)

There, I knew I was right! "The Great Presto Chango presents Books Are Magic at (9:45)."

(to audience)

What time do you have? What??? It *is* (9:45)? Oh, no, I've gotten it backwards again! That's why I'm called Pocus Hocus instead of Hocus Pocus. I get everything backwards. Oooh, what am I going to do now?

(spots cape)

Wait…would you like to see some tricks? I could do them for you. I've always wanted to do the tricks, but the Great Presto Chango only lets me help.

(puts on cape)

And now I, the Prepostifying Pocus Hocus, will perform the Vanishing Wand trick. Do you see this magic wand? You do? I will place it in this newspaper and roll it up, like so. Now I'll say the magic words... uh...

Cadabra-Abra! No, that's not right. Bracadabra! That's not it either.

(responds to audience reaction)

Oh, Abracadabra! That should do it. Now, when I tear up this newspaper, you'll see that the magic wand has disappeared. Tah-dah!

(shows surprise that the trick has worked)

I did it!

For my next trick, I shall pull a rabbit out of this hat.

I'll just say the magic words "Harry Houdini Bustabini." *(nothing happens)*

"Bustabeenie Harry Houdini."

(still nothing; audience response will be "Abracadabra")

See note for poster *in Props Notes, page 32.*

You think I should try "Abracadabra?" Abracadabra!

(checks hat—nothing has happened. looks around, under table, etc.)

RABBIT: *(pops out from behind curtain, taps Pocus Hocus on the back, stays behind her when she jumps and looks to see who is there)*

POCUS HOCUS: Who did that?

(audience responds "The Rabbit")

I know I promised you a rabbit, but I just can't find it anywhere. I really wanted to do a good job, but I can't pull a rabbit out of a hat and I'll never be a good magician, never ever never ever! (wails)

RABBIT: *(taps Pocus Hocus)* Eh…what's up, Doc?

POCUS HOCUS: Where did you come from?

RABBIT: I'm not sure, but let me tell you it was a HARE-raising experience!

POCUS HOCUS: You're supposed to be in the hat.

RABBIT: That's right.

POCUS HOCUS: But you're not!

RABBIT: That's right.

POCUS HOCUS: Well, hurry up and get in there so I can pull you out.

RABBIT: I can't.

POCUS HOCUS: Why not?

RABBIT: I won't fit.

POCUS HOCUS: You've got to fit.

RABBIT: Try me.

POCUS HOCUS: *(gets hat and tries to force Rabbit back in)* Oh, no, what are we going to do?

RABBIT: What do you mean *we*? This isn't my fault.

POCUS HOCUS: You've got to get back in the hat before the Great Presto Chango gets here, or he'll zap me for ruining his magic trick.

RABBIT: Silly apprentice. Don't you know tricks are for kids?

POCUS HOCUS: I was only trying to help. First I made a mistake on the poster, and now this.

RABBIT: *(hands her magic book)* You might try this.

POCUS HOCUS: Yes! *(pages furiously through book, then taps one page triumphantly)* This should do it.

RABBIT: *(reading out of book)* "The wooden handcuffs?" How is that going to get me back in the hat?

POCUS HOCUS: *(tying Rabbit's wrists to broom handle)* It was one of Harry Houdini's most famous tricks. Once you're tied to this stick, I'll cover you with the magic cloth, say the magic words…uh… *(forgets the words, audience responds)* that's right, "Abracadabra" and—"Tah Dah!"—you'll be back in the hat.

RABBIT: Eh… one problem, Doc. That stick won't fit in that hat.

POCUS HOCUS: This is magic! We don't have to worry about that.

RABBIT: As one rabbit said to the other, "We'll play it by ear."

POCUS HOCUS: *(holds cloth in front of Rabbit)* Now, on the count of three, everybody say it with me. Ready? One, two, three... "Abracadabra!" I'm afraid to look. *(removes cloth)*

RABBIT: *(leaning on stick)* Like I said, Doc—tricks are for kids.

POCUS HOCUS: *(uses magic cloth as a crying towel)* I'm a complete failure. I'll never be a magician, and the Great Presto Chango will zap me and nobody will love me and I may as well go out into the garden and eat worms!

RABBIT: *(inspecting hat)* Wait a minute, Doc. What's this? *(pulls library flyer out of hat and reads)* (fill in name of library Reading Club here).

Pocus Hocus: Let me see that. Hey, there are magic words here.

Rabbit: "Bibbety bobbety books"

Pocus Hocus: "Bobbety bookety bibs"

Rabbit: Eh…no, Doc, "Bibbety bobbety books."

Pocus Hocus: Listen!

Rabbit: I'm all ears.

Pocus Hocus: Maybe those are the magic words that will put you back in the hat!

Rabbit: Or maybe they'll put you in hot water. You'd better find out more about them first.

Pocus Hocus: How do I do that?

Rabbit: *(holds out library flyer)* Ahem.

Pocus Hocus: Oh, the brilary! I mean, the library. That's it. We'll go to the library and read some magic books.

Rabbit: They also have newspapers with the want ads, in case you need another job.

Pocus Hocus: But if I read enough about magic, the Great Presto Chango *can't* zap me.

Rabbit: *(reading the flyer)* Hey, Doc, listen to this. Here's a trick even you can do: the Magician's Magic Number Trick.

Pocus Hocus: Magician's Magic Number Trick?

Rabbit: Yeah. You can turn the pages you read into a special prize at the library. All you have to do is read 1000 pages.

Pocus Hocus: That will take forever!

Rabbit: Nah—that's less than ten books. And look here, if you want to take a break from reading you can *(fill in name of library program here)*.

Pocus Hocus: *(reading over Rabbit's shoulder)* OOOH, I want to see *(fill in name of special program here)*. I might learn something there. That does it. I'm going to join the Summer Reading Club and learn all about magic. And if that doesn't help, I think I'll give up magic and join the Babysitters' Club.

Rabbit: Or you could join the "Bunny sitters Club."

Pocus Hocus: *(to audience)* Are you going to join? *(listens to response, then speaks to Rabbit)* I know! Let's go to the library now, and get some books to read while we wait, and find out more about the summer reading club.

Rabbit: *(puts the hat on, and walks arm in arm with Hocus Pocus)* Yeah… I'd like to read a few magic books myself. Who says tricks are just for kids?

Pocus Hocus: Silly Rabbit.

The End

Production Notes

Setting

The skit is set in a school auditorium, where a magic show is about to be performed for the students. The stage curtain should remain closed throughout the skit. All action takes place on the apron, or the area in front of the curtain. If there is a center opening to the curtain, Rabbit will make his entrance there, if not, Rabbit's entrance can be from stage left, but be sure Pocus Hocus keeps his/her back to Rabbit.

The table, covered with a cloth, is set at center stage. The magician's hat is set on the table, as well as the wand, the newspaper, and the fancy shoelaces. All other props are carried in by Pocus Hocus at the beginning of the skit, in a cardboard box if desired.

The poster rests on an easel at far right.

Costumes

For Rabbit: white sweatpants with powder puff tail, white hooded sweatshirt with ears attached, white socks over hands and feet.

Dog Days & Winter Ways

For Pocus Hocus: black skirt or pants, white shirt, red or black bow tie, black jacket (optional), black shoes.

Props

large poster on easel
small table covered with cloth
black magician's hat
library flyer
magician's black cape

calendar
magic wand (made of painted newspaper)
single sheet of newspaper
magic book
wooden pole
fancy shoelaces to tie pole to rabbit
large magic cloth for Wooden Handcuff trick

Props notes

The *poster* can simply be large, easily read letters announcing "The Great Presto Chango presents 'Books Are Magic' at _____." (Fill in the blank with the time of your show reversed. (See page one of script for example.)) If more than one show will be performed, tape the new times over the old ones. If time permits, the poster can be as elaborate and theatrical as you like.

The *table* can be small, even a TV tray will do. It should be covered with a black or blue cloth (or, if you prefer, some bright color) which can be decorated with cut-out stars and moons.

The *black magician's hat* can be purchased at a store which sells party goods. A plastic one is fine.

The *library flyer* can be either a single page or a booklet, as long as it will fit in the hat without being seen from the audience. Tip: Cues or hard-to-remember lines from that part of the skit can be hidden in the program.

The *magician's cape* can be cut out of a piece of black material. Pocus Hocus must fasten it quickly. Velcro is ideal, but short tying strings made of the same cloth and sewn on are fine, too.

Any type of *calendar* or datebook will do—even just a one-month sheet.

The *magic wand* must be made out of a single half-sheet of newspaper rolled up to look like a stick. Paint the middle black and the tips white to make it look authentic. (Tempera or poster paint works well and dries quickly.) Make extras to practice with, and one for each performance.

Only one sheet of *newspaper* is needed for the "Vanishing Wand Trick." If too much paper is used, the trick won't work.

The *magic book* can be one from the library shelves, or a fancy photo album can be used. Tip: Cues can be hidden in here as well as in the program.

An old broomstick without the bristles makes an ideal *wooden pole*. It must be long enough to reach from one of Rabbit's wrists to the other when laid across his shoulders.

The *shoelaces* are used to tie Rabbit to the wooden pole in the Wooden Handcuffs Trick.

The *magic cloth* is held in front of Rabbit during the Wooden Handcuffs Trick, and must be large enough to hide what Rabbit dies behind it. Any type of cloth, decorated or not, will do.

How to perform the magic tricks

The Vanishing Wand Trick

See instructions under Props for making the magic wands. If the wand is not made this way, the trick will not work. Be sure to make extra wands for rehearsals. From the audience, the wand will look real—that is, as if it were made of wood. After flourishing the wand, roll it up in the sheet of newspaper. If too much newspaper is used, the trick will not work.

When Pocus Hocus says the magic words, he/she then tears the rolled up newspaper in half—since the wand is made of painted newspaper, it also tears easily in half while hidden inside the rolled-up newspaper. Pocus Hocus should express surprise when the trick works, as if he/she wasn't certain that it would. Place the two halves of the newspaper in the prop box or on or under the table. Be sure not to unroll it and give the secret away.

The Wooden Handcuffs Trick

Rabbit must stretch out his/her arms to each side. Pocus Hocus puts the wooden pole across Rabbit's shoulders and ties one paw to each end of the pole with the shoelaces. *Rabbit must keep palms open facing the audience while Pocus Hocus ties his wrists to the pole.* Once Pocus Hocus has finished the tying, he/she holds the magic cloth in front of Rabbit. Rabbit then turns wrists so that palms face the ceiling, and uses hands to slide the pole off. Pocus Hocus may have to add a bit of stage business, i.e., forgetting the magic words again, until Rabbit is ready. If Rabbit whispers or gives some sort of signal by poking the cloth, Pocus Hocus will know when it is time to remove the magic cloth. Rabbit should be discovered casually leaning on the wooden pole, hands free, shoelaces still tied to wrists.

7
Station W-Library
By Anne Lemay

A skit for two players

Characters:

BEAR, an overbearing, "Ralph Cramden" type
HARE, an innocent, impish "Ed Norton" type

Setting: *A press booth in the Olympic Arena.*

At rise: Bear *and* Hare *are seated at a broadcast desk.*

HARE: Greetings, out there in TV Land...

BEAR: *(interrupts)* Hsst. Hsst.

HARE: *(urgent undertone)* We're on the air in front of millions of viewers...

BEAR: *(equally urgent undertone)* This is radio.

HARE: What?!!

BEAR: This is radio. Our budget was cut.

HARE: Oh. *(starts again)* Greetings out there in Radio Land...

BEAR: *(interrupts again)* That is so unprofessional.

HARE: What?

BEAR: Starting the show with *(mimicks)* "Greetings out there in Radio Land"! It's so corny I feel like I'm in Kansas, waiting for a twister to whisk me away to the Land of Oz.

HARE: *(thrusts script at Bear)* Here. You do it.

BEAR: I thought you'd never ask. *(speaks in a suave voice)* Hello, Book Fans, you're listening to the *Bear & Hare Show* on station W-LIBRARY, that's W-L-I-B-R-A-R-Y, your reading station on the FM dial. Today we'll be covering an event of olympic proportions...

HARE: *(interrupts)* Don't tell me. The soprano is going to sing.

BEAR: Will you let me do it?

HARE: No sweat. Go for it.

BEAR: *(resuming)* Today we bring you the Summer Reading Olympics. But first, a word from our sponsor.

HARE: *(whispers)* Give me that box.

BEAR: *(whispers back)* I told you, this is radio. No one can see it.

HARE: But it puts me in the reading *moo-d*. *(picks up cereal box and starts commercial)* Does your big brother or sister ever get on your nerves? Do you sometimes wish you could get...*revenge*? Start your day with "We Tease," the cereal guaranteed to make every sibling a monkey's uncle. Test your pest-ability with the help of "We Tease, Breakfast of Chimps."

BEAR: *(sarcastically)* Thank you, Hare.

HARE: I had my We Tease this morning.

BEAR: I can tell.

HARE: So hop to it and start the show already.

BEAR: The events today will kick off with the lighting of the Olympic torch, which has come all the way from Olympia, Greece.

HARE: As far away as that?

BEAR: *(glaring at him)* As far away as that. It has been hand-carried by runners from many nations.

HARE: How did they run over the ocean?

BEAR: *(undertone)* They didn't. A runner flew on a 747 with it.

HARE: Running in place, huh?

BEAR: *(exasperated)* Will you quit running on so?

HARE: I'm not running. But my nose is. *(takes tissue and blows nose)*

BEAR: Very funny.

HARE: Let me run this by you—it's time for another commercial. *(takes sign on pole and begins to jog around desk)* Are you always running late? Don't let time run out. Go for the Gold, with a gold watch from Caldecott Jewelers, the watch that runs in every race. A medal-winner every time.

BEAR: *(sitting with arms folded across chest, watching grimly)* Are you quite through? I suppose running puts you in the mood too. You ran overtime.

HARE: *(suddenly stopping and staring at feet)* Aaaaagh! I killed time! *(drops to knees and begins to feel for the body)* I didn't mean to do it!

BEAR: *(short, clipped tones)* Will. You. Sit. Down. *(Hare sits)*

BEAR: As I was saying, the Olympic torch will be hand-carried into the stadium and used to light the Olympic flame. This year, Tortoise has been given the honor of running with the torch and lighting the flame, at which time...

HARE: *(interrupts)* Tortoise is running? Are you kidding? We'll be here for the next four years!

BEAR: *(coolly)* He beat you in a race, if I recall.

HARE: Yeah, but not because of his running.

BEAR: *(ignores Hare)* As I was saying, Tortoise will carry a torch...

HARE: *(interrupts)* Ooo-ooo, Tortoise is in looooo-ove.

BEAR: What makes you say that?

HARE: He's carrying a torch for someone.

BEAR: *(ignores him again)* A flock of doves will be set free just before the flame is lit...

HARE: They must be love doves.

BEAR: No, they're peace doves.

HARE: Only pieces? Where's the rest of them?

BEAR: *(taking new sheet from script)* While we wait for Tortoise, let's review the line-up of today's events. First, we'll see the 1000 meter Sprint...

HARE: They're going to put money in 1000 parking meters?

BEAR: No, a meter is a unit of measurement.

HARE: You mean they're going past 1000 parking meters?

BEAR: *(exasperated)* No, there are no parking meters!

HARE: Then where will they park their cars?

BEAR: They don't use cars! This is a sprint!

HARE: Oh, Sprint. They're going to put money in the pay phones. I use AT&T. Do you think Sprint is cheaper?

BEAR: No, no, no!! I'm not talking about long distance telephone companies. A sprint is a race. You know, "On your mark, get set, go!"

HARE: Why would I run on Mark? He's my friend.

BEAR: *(pauses, then continues as if Hare had not spoken)* Later today, we'll watch the Hammer Throw...

HARE: They're going to throw M.C. Hammer?

BEAR: *(glares at him, but keeps going)* …and after that the Shot Put.

HARE: Where are they going to put it?

BEAR: *(growls)* In the meters. Will you stop interrupting?

HARE: *(with an angelic smile)* No sweat.

BEAR: The final event of the day is the Discus. *(to Hare)* And, no, they're not going to throw computer disks! As soon as Tortoise arrives the contests will begin.

HARE: Believe me, it's going to be a long wait. The doves are getting restless already. In the meantime, I have a public service announcement.

BEAR: Go ahead. Do you need any cereal boxes, or a little running room?

HARE: Just this. *(blows whistle)*

BEAR: *(covering ears)* Why am I not surprised? *(covers head in arms on desk)*

HARE: *(reading)* On your marks…Get set…*Run down to the library, where you'll discover that reading is no sweat when you join the Summer Reading Club! Kids of all ages are invited to join a reading team and win prizes. Olympic crafts events and special programs will also be held. Don't lag behind the starting gate! Every reader is a winner in (fill in the name of your reading club here).*

BEAR: Let me see that. *(takes script)* Hey, this sounds like fun. Why don't we go down to the library and join?

HARE: Great idea! As soon as Tortoise gets here and the first event starts, we'll do that.

BEAR: *(muttering)* Come on, Tortoise.

HARE: Anyone out there got a match?

BEAR: Hare, we can't do that!

HARE: Do what?

BEAR: Were you planning on lighting the Olympic flame with a match?

HARE: (holds up sneaker) No, I was looking for a match to my sneaker so I could run down to the library. Anyway, the doves are still there. If we light the flame before they're let go, we'd have free fried lunch.

BEAR: Yuck. (taps fingers on desk impatiently) Where is that reptile?

HARE: Well, if you're going to call him names, don't leave out pond scum.

BEAR: Let's not split hairs, Hare.

HARE: Bear with me! I have an idea! Here. *(hands Bear a cassette)*

BEAR: What, is this tape due back at the library?

HARE: No, but our fans can listen to the music while we sprint over to the library to join the Summer Reading Club! We can pick up a few books to read on the air while we wait for Tortoise and the torch, too.

BEAR: *(suave voice)* Book fans, for your listening pleasure, the *Bear & Hare Show* on Station W-LIBRARY on your FM dial, now brings you music for olympic reading.

HARE: It's a Reading Marathon! Ready…Set…READ! *(music starts as Bear & Hare leave broadcast desk)*

BEAR: That was brilliant.

HARE: No sweat. May they all read hoppily ever after. *(hops offstage)*

BEAR: *(running to catch up)* Don't leave a bear behind!

The End

Production Notes

Setting

The skit is set in a press booth at the Olympic Arena. The background area should be simple and uncluttered. If performed on a school stage, no background scenery is necessary, but if there is equipment, etc., on stage, it might be best to perform in front of the closed curtain. This skit is especially successful if performed in the school gym. A library or classroom performance will serve just as well if the area immediately behind Hare and Bear is relatively empty and won't distract the audience.

Costumes

For Hare: a white sweatsuit, with a pom-pom tail sewn onto the seat. Ears can be made of cloth or paper and worn on a headband. He/she only wears one sneaker.

For Bear: a brown or black sweatsuit, also with cloth or paper ears to match. The nose can be blackened with make-up.

Props

broadcast desk
microphone
script or loose sheets of paper
"We Tease" cereal box
Caldecott Jewelers sign on short pole
whistle
sneaker
tape player
audiocassette

Props Notes

The *broadcast desk* is any rectangular table or desk with two chairs. Use a real *microphone*, since most schools and libraries have one, and it will also serve to amplify your voice. Your copies of the *script* for this skit can double as props. The *We Tease cereal box* can be made from an actual box of cereal—just cover the manufacturer's name with a label which reads "WE TEASE." Use oaktag or cardboard to make a *sign for "Caldecott Jewelers."* Be sure the letters are big and can be seen from the back of the audience. The sign can be attached to a wooden dowel or carried in both hands. Any standard *whistle* should be used. Wear it around your neck if you prefer. The *sneaker* can be the match to the one Hare is wearing or a mismatch—either very large or very small. A standard audio *tape player* should be on the broadcast desk. Be sure to supply it with batteries in case the power cord won't reach an electrical outlet. Play a favorite *audiocassette* tape as Hare and Bear exit. We used the music of Scott Joplin, which is rhythmic and bouncy, providing an upbeat ending. You may have a favorite song which will work just as well.

8
Three Ring Reading
By Anne Lemay

A skit for two players

Characters:

COTTON CANDY CLOWN, a happy-go-lucky, light-hearted type

CHLORINE CLOWN, a bossy, know-it-all type

Setting: *A small cooking tent just outside the circus big top.*

At rise: *A table, covered with a tablecloth, is at center stage. A box of props is set on a smaller table or chair just to the left of it. A tiny basket or box, a club, a ringmaster's top hat and whistle are pre-set beneath the table.* Cotton Candy Clown *enters left and crosses downstage.*

COTTON CANDY: *(to audience)* Ringling Brothers and Barnum and Bailey! Am I ever excited! It's the Bearded Lady's birthday, and Chlorine Clown and I are going to make her a cake! *(rummages in prop box)* Now, let's see… first we need a recipe. Ah, here it is! *(holds up cookbook)* This cookbook has been with the circus for 100 years. I have to be very careful with it. *(flips through the pages, which are blank—it's a magic book)* Jumping jugglers! What am I to do? Someone has erased all the recipes. *(shows audience)* Look! Do you see anything written here? *(audience responds)* Neither do I! Wait! Maybe I need my glasses. *(puts on a pair of ridiculous eyeglasses)* Now let me look again. *(flips book again, from the opposite side so that the pages are filled—see Production Notes)* Oh, that's better. I see them now, do you? *(shows audience)* What a relief!

CHLORINE: *(stomps on, cracking a whip)* If that don't beat all! What does he think we are, clowns or something? *(cracks whip again, then notices Cotton Candy)* What are *you* looking at? *(cracks whip)*

COTTON CANDY: *(jumps to escape whip)* Heh, heh. Cool whip. *(jumps as Chlorine cracks it once more)*

CHLORINE: What does he think we have, whipped cream for brains? Do you know what the ringmaster did? *(cracks whip)*

COTTON CANDY: *(jumps)* He played "Crack the Whip?"

CHLORINE: No! He went shopping with the Bearded Lady. For her birthday present! And it's time for the show to start!

COTTON CANDY: *(doesn't get it)* So why don't we do the show without the Bearded Lady?

CHLORINE: *(mimics)* Of course we can "do the show without the Bearded Lady," but we can't… do… the show… without… the ringmaster! *(leans over Cotton Candy and raises her voice as she speaks)*

COTTON CANDY: *(looks at Chlorine, then sits down and weeps loudly)* Waaaaaaaa! *(takes tablecloth from table and blows nose in it)*

CHLORINE: It's no use crying over it. The show must go on.

COTTON CANDY: *(wails)* I'm not crying over that!

CHLORINE: Well, why are you crying?

Cotton Candy: I'm crying because you yelled at me!

Chlorine: Stop wasting time and help me figure out what to do.

Cotton Candy: *(stops crying immediately)* All right. Just a minute. *(stands, shakes out tablecloth, polishes it on her rear end, and replaces it on table, setting mixing bowl on top)* What do we do?

Chlorine: Somebody has to act as ringmaster, and during the acts we'll both make the cake.

Cotton Candy: So, who's going to act as ringmaster? *(Chlorine looks out at audience as if to pick a volunteer, then points finger at Cotton Candy)* Oh, no! No, no, no, no, no!

Chlorine: It's easy! There's nothing to it. *(thrusts whip at Cotton Candy)*

Cotton Candy: What am I supposed to say?

Chlorine: *(mimics while handing hat and whistle to Cotton Candy)* "What am I supposed to say?" You say what every ringmaster says.

Cotton Candy: I say what every ringmaster says. Well, every night at supper our ringmaster says, "Please pass the salt." Shall I say that?

Chlorine: Look. *(takes back hat, whip, and whistle)* You do this. *(blows whistle)* Ladies and Gentlemen, and Children of all ages! *(cracks whip)* Get it?

Cotton Candy: Got it.

Chlorine: Good. *(gives back props)* Now do it.

Cotton Candy: *(blows whistle)* Ladies and Gentlemen, and Children of all ages… please pass the salt!!! *(cracks whip)*

Chlorine: No, that's not it.

Cotton Candy: You *said* "Ladies and Gentlemen!"

Chlorine: But you don't say "pass the salt."

Cotton Candy: You forgot to say "please!"

Chlorine: *(pushes Cotton Candy toward exit)* Just get out there and act like a ringmaster. *(calls after her)* The lion tamer is on first!

Cotton Candy: *(exiting right)* Who's on second?

Chlorine: *(picks up cookbook)* Now the cake. Hmmm, we'll need a recipe…*(finds one)* Aha! this will do! "Three Ring Circus Cake." You make three cakes and pile one on top of the other—sort of like a big top! *(reads from cookbook)* "First add salt"—*(groans)* salt again! *(rummages in prop box for salt and pours in bowl)* *(Cotton Candy tiptoes in with finger on lips to stand secretly behind Chlorine)*

Chlorine: *(reading recipe)* "Three fingers of flour." *(pulls flowers from prop box with three fingers)* Ta-dah! *(dumps them in bowl while Cotton Candy shakes head)* "Sugar to taste." *(takes sugar bowl from box and tastes sugar with finger)* Hmm. Not bad. *(replaces sugar without adding any to bowl)* "One apple, cut in two." *(takes apple and cleaver from prop box and prepares to chop)*

Cotton Candy: Do you know what side of the apple is the reddest?

Chlorine: *(startled)* What!

Cotton Candy: The outside.

Chlorine: What are you doing here?

Cotton Candy: *(points off right)* I don't want to be there.

Chlorine: What about the circus?

Cotton Candy: Well, I was going to have the lion tamer introduce the acts, but the lion is having a bad hair day.

Chlorine: And?

Cotton Candy: He ate the lion tamer.

Chlorine: So what are the people watching?

Cotton Candy: *(innocently)* They're watching the lion chew.

CHLORINE: Quick! Send in the clowns! You're supposed to send in the clowns when something goes wrong!

COTTON CANDY: *(gestures toward bowl)* But we're the clowns, and we're busy. I know! I'll send in the elephants. They can work the peanut gallery.

CHLORINE: Wait! They'll need this. *(hands Cotton Candy a trick can of peanuts)*

COTTON CANDY: Peanuts! Oh, I'll have some first. *(opens can—a spring snake jumps out—grabs it and exits right with can)*

CHLORINE: Maybe she should use the snake charmer, too. Oh, well. *(reads recipe)* "One cup of water." *(takes cup from prop box and dips into bucket on floor)* This water isn't so dirty. *(holding it high, pours into bowl)* "One chocolate chip." *(rummages for it in box, drops in bowl)* "One egg." *(finds in box)* I hope a plastic one will do. This is going to be the best birthday cake ever!

COTTON CANDY: *(enters right)* Okay, Chlorine, everything's set. The elephants and the seals are performing together.

CHLORINE: Why is that?

COTTON CANDY: The elephants wanted their act "sealed with a kiss." *(makes kissing noises)* What's next?

CHLORINE: How about the snake charmer?

COTTON CANDY: I mean what's next with the cake. What can I do to help?

CHLORINE: It says to "beat vigorously."

COTTON CANDY: Oh, I couldn't do that.

CHLORINE: What do you mean, *(mimics)* "Oh, I couldn't do that"? Of course you can do that.

COTTON CANDY: If you say so. *(picks up club and beats Chlorine)*

CHLORINE: Not me, you clown! The cake!

COTTON CANDY: Oh! *(begins beating cake with club)*

CHLORINE: No, no, no! Like this! *(takes club, almost uses it to mix, tosses it aside, stirs with spoon three times, and presents to Cotton Candy)* Ta-dah!

COTTON CANDY: *(tastes batter with finger)* It doesn't taste right.

CHLORINE: *(tasting)* You're right. Something's wrong. *(rummages in prop box and pulls out spider)* This should do it. *(adds spider to bowl and stirs three times)*

COTTON CANDY: *(tasting)* No, it still needs something. *(rummages in box, pulls out long pearl necklace, adds to bowl and stirs three times)*

CHLORINE: *(tastes)* Not quite. *(rummages in box, pulls out mouse and dangles it over bowl before dropping it in and stirring batter three times)* Ta-Dah!

COTTON CANDY: *(to audience)* You expect me to taste that?

AUDIENCE: *(who will respond without prompting!)* Yes!!!!

COTTON CANDY: *(tastes and pauses)* Almost. Wait. *(retrieves club)* Try this.

CHLORINE: *(makes face, but stirs with club three times and tastes)* That's it!

COTTON CANDY: *(tastes)* That's it!

CHLORINE: Hey! What about the circus? The seals must be puckered out by now.

COTTON CANDY: The next act! *(retrieves tiny basket from under table)*

CHLORINE: What's that?

COTTON CANDY: The next act! Henrietta Louise and her Circus of Fleas!

CHLORINE: *(takes basket)* There's only one flea in there.

COTTON CANDY: That's Henrietta Louise.

CHLORINE: Where's her Circus of Fleas?

Cotton Candy: Unfortunately, there was an accident. They fell out of the basket.

Chlorine: That's too bad.

Cotton Candy: Fortunately, there was a haystack beneath them.

Chlorine: That's good.

Cotton Candy: Unfortunately, there was a pitchfork in the haystack.

Chlorine: That's bad.

Cotton Candy: Fortunately, they missed the pitchfork.

Chlorine: That's good.

Cotton Candy: Unfortunately, they also missed the haystack.

Chlorine: That's bad.

Cotton Candy: Fortunately, they landed on a dog, and he's been itching to see them ever since. *(scratches)* It was a hair-raising experience. *(to Audience)* Would you like to see Henrietta Louise perform her tricks? *(takes pretend flea from basket)* Okay, Henrietta Louise, on the count of three jump in a circle. One, two, three! *(Cotton Candy and Chlorine move their heads in a circle as if watching the flea)* Very good! *(to Audience)* Did you see that? No? Henrietta Louise, jump in a square this time. Are you ready? One, two, three! *(Both move heads in square pattern)* You didn't see that either? Henrietta Louise, you're going to have to do the hardest trick of all. *(to Audience)* On the count of three Henrietta Louise will jump from my hand all the way to the ceiling and back! One, two, three! *(Both follow flea's path to ceiling, then look around distractedly)* Henrietta Louise? Where are you? *(Cotton Candy looks suddenly at bowl)* Oh, no! Henrietta Louise has fallen into the cake and she can't get up! What are we going to do?

Chlorine: What are we going to do? Beats me! *(looks in basket)*

Cotton Candy: *(picking up club)* I don't see how that will help. *(raises club to beat Chlorine but never makes contact)*

Chlorine: Wait! What's this? *(takes tiny note out of basket)* *(fill in name of reading club here)* Hey, it's a message from the library.

Cotton Candy: The fleas must have sent it to Henrietta Louise. Poor Henrietta! What does it say?

Chlorine: *(reads)* "Dear Henrietta Louise, We're at *(fill in name of library here)* and we've joined the summer reading club. We are earning prizes just for reading books. There are lots of fun programs, too. We hope you can meet us there. Love, the Fleas."

Cotton Candy: Maybe we should join the reading club. We could read books between acts!

Chlorine: We could go to some of these programs, too. Look, there's *(fill in names of special activities here)*.

Cotton Candy: I want to go to *(fill in name of program here)*

Chlorine: Let's go to the library now and join the reading club.

Cotton Candy: We can look for a book about rescuing a drowning flea, too!

Chlorine: Hang on to that chocolate chip, Henrietta Louise! Let's go, Cotton Candy.

Cotton Candy: Wait! My mother always told me never leave with the stove on. I'll just use this bucket of water to put it out. *(picks up bucket and empties on first row of audience—confetti falls out instead of water)* *(Both clowns exit left with exaggerated steps)*

The End

Production Notes

Setting

The skit is set in the cook tent of a circus at showtime. The action may take place in front of the closed curtain on an auditorium stage, but leaving the curtain open will allow the actors to enter and exit upstage, giving added depth to the playing area.

A table, covered with a colorful tablecloth, is downstage center. A small card table may be used, but a sturdy snack tray will be less cumbersome. A chair, stool, or smaller table just to the left of the center table holds a colorful prop box. The tiny basket, the club, and the Ringmaster's hat and whistle are preset beneath the table.

Costumes

Since both Chlorine and Cotton Candy are clowns just about anything is appropriate dress, from traditional clown costumes to a hodge podge look created from your own closet. The sillier you look the better! The clowns can be male instead of female—feel free to rename them. Think colorful, think layers (shirts on top of shirts, or three ties), and think silly! In our production, Chlorine wore a purple petticoat, a leotard, and had her hair in a topknot. Cotton Candy wore white tights, white shorts and shirt, a colorful tie and a silly hat. Both clowns wore minimal makeup. It is a good idea to do some accenting with makeup, such as whiteface or red circles on the cheeks or nose, to help the clowns look out of the ordinary, but elaborate face makeup isn't necessary.

Props

tiny basket for fleas
tiny note
club
Ringmaster's hat and whistle
parasol
large mixing bowl
mixing spoon
trick cookbook
eyeglasses
whip
box of salt
plastic flowers
sugar bowl
apple
cleaver
trick peanut can
cup
bucket of confetti
Waldo's hat
plastic egg
spider
pearl necklace
stuffed mouse

Props Notes

The *tiny basket* can be anything small—an empty gift box for jewelry will do. The fleas, of course, are imaginary! The *tiny note* may be cut from any type of paper, and should be about 2"x2". Tip: You can actually write the letter from the fleas on the note, and eliminate the need to memorize it! The *club* can be a soft foam toy or a plastic baseball bat. The *Ringmaster's hat* is found in party stores but can be eliminated if you don't find one. A real top hat would look great! Any standard *whistle* will be fine. Put it on a chain or a ribbon for easier handling. The *parasol* should be doll-sized to create a silly effect, but also can be eliminated if not available.

The *large mixing bowl* might just turn up in your kitchen! Tupperware makes one, but stainless steel bowls are available from restaurant supply stores and discount warehouses. Try to borrow either type from someone if you don't own one. The *mixing spoon* can be a standard wooden one, or something oversized or tiny. Try using a mini egg whisk for a comic effect!

Our *trick cookbook* was a cereal box giveaway and was actually a comic book, not a cookbook. Trick books of this type are available in magic shops. If you want to make your own, alternate blank pages with pages which have pictures or text on them. Cut the blank pages one-quarter inch longer than the others. Once they are bound, flipping the pages from back to front will reveal a different set of pages than when flipping from front to back.
The *eyeglasses* may be borrowed from a child's doll, or you might decide to use zany ones with

eyeballs falling out, or giant-sized glasses. Party stores, costume shops, and even discount department stores may have something special, but check your child's closet first. The *whip* can be salvaged from a Halloween costume, or use ribbon or rawhide strips on a stick wrapped with black tape.

The items which go into the bowl are easy to find or adapt. A salt shaker may be used instead of the *box of salt*, and silk *flowers* instead of plastic ones. The *sugar bowl* can be a bag or box labelled "sugar." Use a real *apple* or a plastic one. The *cleaver* was an old Halloween prop, and looks very funny on stage. Since it was plastic, there was no danger of an accidental cut while rummaging through the prop box. If such an item isn't available for you, use a plastic knife (i.e., the type which comes with fast food) but exaggerate your movements as if you were using a cleaver.

The *trick peanut can* is available from magic shops or gag stores, but can be eliminated if not available.

We used a plastic *cup* with a lid so that the water wouldn't spill in the prop box. Since the *bucket* holds confetti, the water must be preset in the cup. Chlorine Clown must take the lid off while the cup is still in the prop box and hold the cup upright at all times, even when dipping it into the bucket. The audience is truly convinced that the bucket is filled with water. It isn't necessary to fill the bucket with confetti. The custodians will appreciate it if you merely cover the bottom of the bucket and the surprise will still be effective.

Waldo's hat is a red and white ski cap, just like the one he wears in the books by Martin Handford. If the Waldo books aren't popular in your library or you are unable to find a ski cap like that, just eliminate that bit of stage business. You may want to substitute something else which will immediately be identified with a literary character (such as Rapunzel's hair or Cinderella's shoe).

The reason for using a *plastic egg* is to avoid the mess made by a broken one. If you want to use a hard-boiled egg, go ahead. The large eggs which contain pantyhose or colored plastic eggs which are sold for the Easter holidays will be effective.

The *spider* must be large enough to be seen from the back of the audience. A large rubber one works best, but if you have a spider hand puppet that will do the job also. Avoid the tiny plastic ones, which are often attached to rings or earrings, unless your audience will be very small. Feel free to substitute any gruesome item you find!

The *pearl necklace* was chosen just because it was a silly thing to put in a cake. At some performances, Cotton Candy held the necklace over the bowl and then put it on instead of adding it to the cake, saying, "I'll bet you thought I was going to put that in the cake, didn't you?" Any long necklace may be substituted, or something entirely different, like an old shoe or a necktie.

The *stuffed mouse* was a child's toy. A rubber cat toy will work equally well, but be sure it looks like a mouse or rat and can be easily seen from the back of the audience. Of course, you may use something different if a *mouse* isn't available, but this did bring the biggest reaction from the audience.

Appendix A
Contacting Performance Sites

If you are working in a public library, you may want to promote your summer reading program by performing a skit in the local schools. A phone call to the school librarian may be all you need to set up a visit if you already have a working relationship with each other.

Unless this is the case, however, a letter sent to the school librarian, with a copy sent to the principal, will give you a chance to introduce yourself and your purpose. (A sample letter is included on page 46.) Be sure to include the best times for them to call you, to avoid playing telephone tag. Do follow up with a phone call yourself if they don't respond to your letter.

Many communities have a library coordinator or supervising librarian. If this is the situation in your community, try that person first. He or she may be able to smooth the way for you. Be sure each letter is addressed to an individual and not "Dear School Librarian." A phone call to the office of the Superintendent of Schools will give you the names and titles you need. Your letter should be typed on the library's letterhead stationery.

Library Letterhead

Date

Mrs. Marge Mazaitis
Librarian
Eisenhower School
Piscataway, Nj 08854

Dear Mrs. Mazaitis:

The theme for Piscataway Public Library's summer reading club is Three Ring Reading, and it promises a circusful of fun and prizes for children who read this summer.

We have prepared a skit to promote the reading club, and we'd like to perform it at Eisenhower School. It features two clowns backstage at a circus who find out about the reading club and decide to join. The skit lasts about fifteen minutes, and we'd like to answer any questions the students have about the reading club after the performance.

We've set aside the week of June 14th for performances, but we are willing to consider other dates if this isn't convenient. You can reach me at 463-1633 from 9:30 am until 5:00 pm on Mondays, Wednesdays, and Thursdays. The best time to call is 10:00 - 11:30 am or after 3:00 pm.

I look forward to hearing from you!

Sincerely,

Anne Lemay
Librarian
Children's Services

Appendix B
Stage Areas

Stage directions for actors are always given from the actor's perspective. All playing areas on a stage are referred to in this way. When the actor stands at center stage facing the audience, "upstage" is behind him, "downstage" before him, "stage left" to *his* left, and "stage right" to *his* right. This means that the *actor's* left is actually the *audience's* right.

You might wonder why there is an "upstage" and a "downstage" section when the floor of the stage is usually flat. At one time, theater stages were built on a slant, or "raked," with the lowest part nearest the audience. The terms upstage and downstage are a remnant of that era.

As a result of this, stage right may also be upstage, center or downstage (often abbreviated using initials, i.e., D.R. for Down Right), and so on for stage left and center.

The "apron" is the part of the stage in front of the main curtain which traditionally opens or closes to begin and end the play. The "wings" are off the stage to the side. Most entrances and exits are made from or to the "wings." The illustration on the next page is included to give you a quick reference to the stage areas.

Stage Areas

The Stage (seen from above)

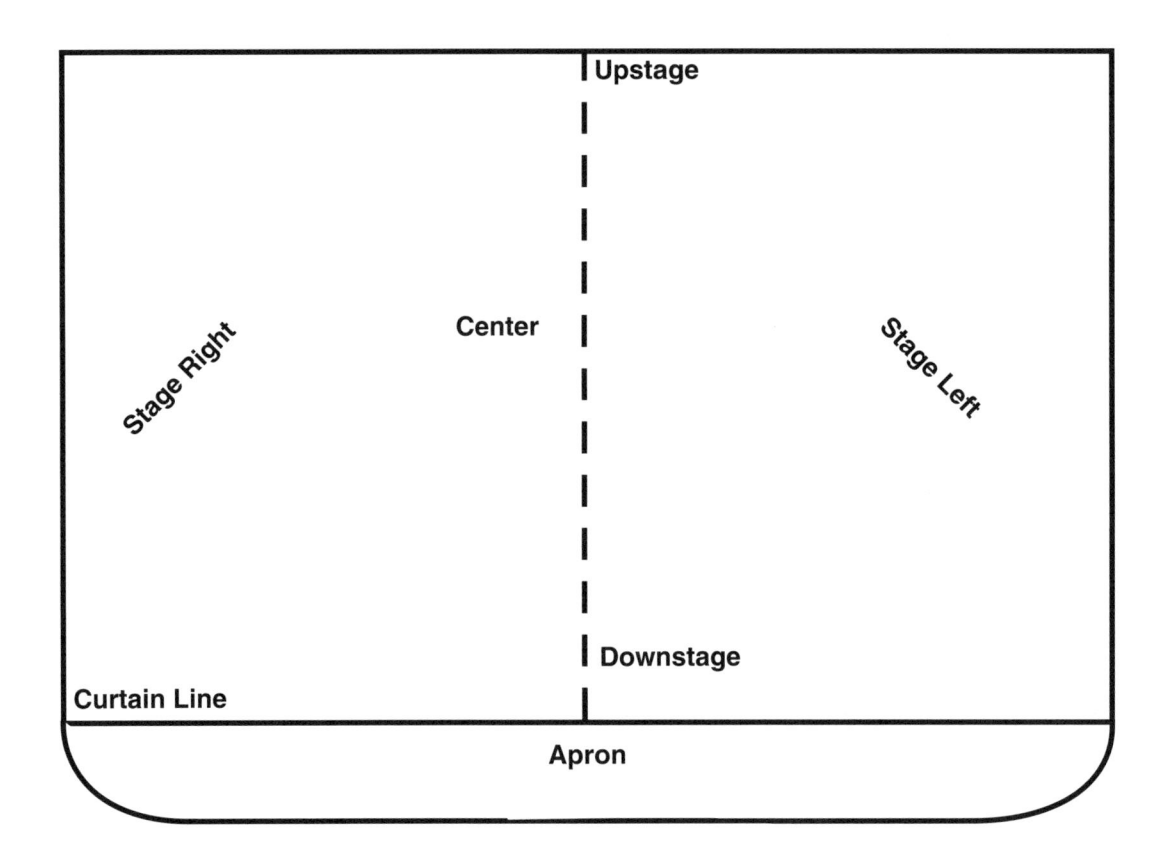

```
┌─────────────────────────────────────────┐
│                    | Upstage            │
│                    |                    │
│                    |                    │
│                    |                    │
│   Stage Right   Center  |   Stage Left  │
│                    |                    │
│                    |                    │
│                    |                    │
│                    | Downstage          │
│ Curtain Line       |                    │
└────────────────── Apron ────────────────┘
```

Audience

Appendix C
Glossary

actor—a performer in a stage play.

at rise—at the beginning of the play, when the curtain (if one is being used) rises.

cast—the actors who perform in a play; or the process of choosing which actors will portray which characters.

character—someone in a skit or play, with qualities, habits or characteristics that make him/her a unique individual.

cheating—facing the audience with at least three-quarters of the body rather than looking at the actor to whom you are speaking on the stage.

clown—a comedian; someone who makes others laugh by saying or doing something funny.

costumes—the clothing worn by actors in a play.

countercross—the movement of an actor from one place on the stage to another at the same time that another actor is crossing.

cross—the movement of an actor from one place on the stage to another.

cue—the lines or stage business which signal another actor's lines or stage business.

delivery—the manner or style of speaking used by an actor while performing in a play.

dialogue—the words spoken by the actors in a play.

discovery—the moment when a clown or an actor sees something, realizes something, or gets an idea for solving a problem in a play.

dress rehearsal—a final rehearsal for a play in which everything is exactly as it will be during the performance.

energy level—the excitement an actor uses while performing in a play, including timing and pace.

entrance—the appearance of an actor on the stage.

exit—the departure of an actor from the stage.

hamming it up—using a showy, over-exaggerated style in presenting a character on the stage.

hook—a gimmick, or something upon which the action or motivation in a play revolves.

improvisation—a scene or situation which is made up on the spot, without prior rehearsal or written dialogue.

lines—the words or dialogue spoken by an actor in a play.

lose the audience—to lose the attention of those who are watching the play.

monologue—a long speech by one actor in a play.

motivation—the reason a character does a particular action or speaks a particular line on the stage.

objective—what the character in a play wants.

pace—the speed and timing at which a play is performed.

production—the process of putting on a play.

props—an abbreviated term for "stage properties," which are any objects used or carried by the actors on stage.

proscenium stage—a stage which has a "frame" between the apron and the playing area to separate the audience from the actors.

read-through—the first reading of a play by the entire cast, usually at the first rehearsal.

rehearsal—the practice of a play before performing.

role—the character portrayed by an actor.

scenery—the background decorations which give an idea of where a play is taking place.

script—the written dialogue and stage directions of a play.

setting—the time and place of the action in a play.

skit—a short play which is usually funny.

stage—the area used by the actors when a play is performed.

stage directions—the description, sometimes abbreviated and always in parentheses, of where an actor is to move on the stage.

stage fright—a fear of performing in front of others, or of forgetting the lines one's character is supposed to speak.

staging—the process of putting on a play.

straight man—one who acts as a contrast for a comedian or clown; a stooge.

timing—the speed at which something is performed.

type casting—assigning roles to actors based on their physical appearance or the type of personality they usually portray.

00135 0704